THE BOOK OF
Hot & Spicy
NIBBLES — DIPS — DISHES

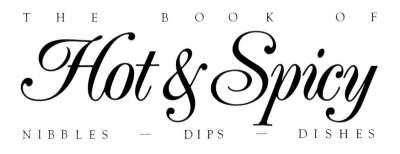

THE BOOK OF
Hot & Spicy
NIBBLES — DIPS — DISHES

LOUISE STEELE

Photography by
PAUL GRATER

TED SMART

Specially produced for Ted Smart,
Guardian House, Borough Road,
Godalming, Surrey GU7 2AE.

This book was created by Merehurst Limited,
Ferry House, 51/57 Lacy Road, Putney, London SW15 1PR.

©Copyright Merehurst Limited 1987

ISBN: 1 85613 180 7

Managing Editor: Felicity Jackson
Designer: Roger Daniels
Home Economist: Anne Hildyard
Photographer: Paul Grater
Typeset by Angel Graphics
Colour separation by J. Film Process Ltd, Bangkok, Thailand.
Printed in Belgium by Proost International Book Production, Turnhout

ACKNOWLEDGEMENTS

The publishers would like to thank the following for their
help and advice:

David Mellor, 26 James Street, Covent Garden, London WC2E 8PA,
4 Sloane Square, London SW1W 8EE and
66 King Street, Manchester M2 4NP
Elizabeth David Limited, 46 Bourne Street, London SW1 and at
Covent Garden Kitchen Supplies, 3 North Row, The Market,
London WC2
Lawleys Limited, 154 Regent Street, London W1R 6LA
Napkins from a selection at The White House, 51-52 New Bond
Street, London W1
Neal Street East, the Oriental specialist, 5 Neal Street,
Covent Garden, London WC2
Pages, Trade Catering Suppliers, 121 Shaftesbury Avenue, London WC2
Philips Home Appliances, City House, 420-430 London Road,
Croydon CR9 3QR

Notes:
All spoon measurements are equal.
1 teaspoon = 5 ml spoon.
1 tablespoon = 15 ml spoon.

CONTENTS

INTRODUCTION

Variety is said to be the spice of life – and, whereas, for many millions of people throughout the world life has been a variety of spices for centuries, it's only thanks to early explorers, who returned home with shiploads of exotic spices, that Western culinary art was transformed.

The Book of Hot and Spicy Nibbles, Dips & Dishes has over 100 beautifully illustrated step-by-step recipes which include traditional favourites like Steak au Poivre, Mexican Chilli con Carne, Indonesian Gado Gado and Creole Jambalaya, plus many Indian and oriental dishes and lots of sizzling new surprises and variations on a theme. Whether you are looking for a simple snack; a teatime treat, or an elegant dinner party dish, this book has a recipe for all occasions.

Spices are invaluable for adding that special blend of heat, or fragrance and pungency to all manner of savoury and sweet dishes. Don't be daunted by those unfamiliar to you – try them, or you'll never know what you've been missing, but bear in mind that some are stronger and more fiery than others. If experimenting, it is wise to start with small amounts – you can always add more to taste at a later stage. And remember – the amount of spices in many of the following recipes are suggested as a guide, so feel free to increase or decrease the amounts according to personal preference.

It is the chilli (in its various forms) that adds heat to a dish, and you will find instructions on how to prepare this fiery spice (without getting burnt!), plus many recipes using it. There is also plenty of information on all the other hot spices – mustard, pepper, cloves and ginger – plus the more fragrant, aromatic ones like cardamom, cumin and nutmeg.

The following recipes range from the mild to hot, or just wonderfully spicy. It is a collection to please hot and spicy food-lovers everywhere . . . and is tempting enough to persuade the 'uninitiated' to sample the delights of spicy foods!

CHILLIES

Chillies belong to the pepper (capsicum) family, as do sweet peppers but there the relationship ends, for the fiery heat of the chilli is in no way similar to its mild-flavoured relation. Fresh chillies are now widely available and vary considerably in size, shape and heat factor. In principle, the fatter chillies tend to be more mild than the long, thin varieties, and the smaller the chilli, the hotter its taste. Generally, the unripened, green chilli is less fiery than when ripened and red, but there are exceptions according to the variety, so it is wise to remember that all chillies, irrespective of colour, shape and size, are hot, so use caution before adding them to a dish. Bear in mind that a little chilli goes a long way, so add a small amount to begin with and gradually increase the quantity to your liking during cooking.

Take care when preparing chillies – the tiny, cream-coloured seeds inside are the hottest part and, in general, are removed before using. Chillies contain a pungent oil which can cause an unpleasant burning sensation to eyes and skin, so it's a wise precaution to wear rubber gloves when handling chillies and to be sure not to touch your face or eyes during preparation. Cut off stalk end, then split open the pod and scrape out seeds, using a pointed knife. Discard the seeds. Rinse pods thoroughly under cold running water and pat dry before chopping or slicing as required. Once this task is completed, wash hands, utensils and surfaces with soapy water.

Dried red chillies are sold whole and can vary in size from 1-2 cm (½-¾ in) to 4-5 cm (1½-2 in) in length, so take this into account when using. If a recipe states small dried chillies, and you only have the larger ones, reduce the quantity accordingly. Dried chillies are usually soaked in hot water for 1 hour before draining and removing seeds (as described left), unless a recipe states otherwise.

Dried red chillies, when ground, are used to make cayenne pepper and, combined with other spices and seasonings, also make chilli and curry powder, and chilli seasoning. They are also used in the making of Tabasco and chilli sauce.

The Harissa spice mix, see page 13, uses a large quantity of dried chillies and is very hot, so be warned! This is a favourite spice mix for many Middle Eastern dishes. Don't be tempted to add more Harissa than recipe states, unless you are prepared for an extremely hot dish. A less fiery Harissa can be made simply by removing the seeds from soaked chillies, before crushing with other ingredients.

Green chillies are available canned in brine. These are often ready-seeded and peeled and taste pleasantly hot and spicy – ideal for adding to pizza toppings, sauces and taco fillings. Both red and green chillies also come pickled in jars (hot or mild/sweet) and can be found in specialist delicatessens and ethnic food shops. Canned and pickled varieties should be drained and patted dry before using. Whether you seed the pickled type is up to you, just remember the seeds are the hottest part!

MUSTARD

White or yellow, brown and black seeds all come from the mustard plant, according to the species. Most commonly found is the creamy yellow type (this is the one used to produce 'mustard and cress') which is the least pungent. The brown type (or Indian mustard) is stronger in flavour, while the black mustard seed is the most powerful of all. The creamy yellow seeds are more widely available, but look out for the black and brown types in Asian and Oriental food shops and specialist delicatessens.

Whole mustard seeds have a pleasant nutty bite to them and can be used to add piquancy to salad dressing and hot sauces – especially good when served with fish, chicken and pork. They are also delicious added to coleslaw and creamy potato salads and are a popular addition to pickles and chutneys. Use mustard seeds (especially the two hotter varieties) with discretion to begin with, increasing the amount as you become more familiar with the flavours.

It is the yellow seed, processed with

black seeds, wheat flour and turmeric, which forms the basis of English mustard. Mustard powder can be used as it is in cooking, or may be mixed to a paste with a little cold or warm water. (For a richer mixture, it can be mixed with a little cream or milk). Once mixed it should be left for at least 10 minutes to allow time for the flavours to develop. It is only when the powder is mixed with a liquid that the essential oils are released, giving mustard its pungency and sensation of heat. Remember that made mustard loses its pungency after a few hours. Jars of prepared mustards, once opened, need using up within a few weeks as the flavour and colour will deteriorate.

The variety of ready-prepared mustards come in a bewildering number of mouthwatering flavours. These can be made from milled mustard flour, or from coarsely crushed seed (the proportions of which vary tremendously, depending on the type). Some are mixed with vinegar, others with grape juice or wine (and sometimes beer) and often contain various spices, herbs and seasonings, such as honey and horseradish. German mustard, which is mild and sweet-flavoured, is a mixture of brown and white mustard flour, moistened with vinegar and flavoured with various spices. The mild-flavoured American mustard (popular with children) generally uses only yellow mustard seeds with the addition of sugar, vinegar and salt. Dijon mustard, made from milled, dehusked black seeds, is flavoured with wine and spices. The pungent and spicy grainy types of mustard are a mixture of whole, crushed black and yellow seeds with additional flavourings added for individuality.

Mustards of all types can be used to great effect, not only as a condiment, but also as a culinary ingredient. They add bite and piquancy to all manner of savoury dishes from scrambled eggs, sauces and dressings, to devilled mixtures, barbecued foods, soups, casseroles, pastry or scones.

A–Z OF SPICES

Allspice (1) These small, dark, reddish-brown berries are so called because their aroma and flavour resembles a combination of cinnamon, cloves and nutmeg. Use berries whole in marinades; for boiling and pot-roasting meats and poultry; in fish dishes, pickles and chutneys. Also available ground and excellent for flavouring milk puddings and cakes.

Anise (2) Commonly called aniseed, these small, brown oval seeds have the sweet, pungent flavour of liquorice. Also available ground. Use seeds in stews and vegetable dishes, or scatter over loaves and rolls before baking. Try ground anise for flavouring fish dishes and pastries for fruit pies.

Caraway (3) Small, brown crescent-shaped seeds with a strong liquorice flavour and especially delicious as a flavouring in braised cabbage and sauerkraut recipes. Also in breads.

Cardamom (4) Small, triangular-shaped pods containing numerous small black seeds which have a warm, highly aromatic flavour. You can buy green or black cardamoms, although green are more widely available.

Cayenne (5) Orangey-red in colour, this ground pepper is extremely hot and pungent. Not to be confused with paprika, which, although related, is mild-flavoured.

Chilli powder (6) Made from dried red chillies. This red powder varies in flavour and hotness, from mild to hot. A less fiery type is found in chilli seasoning.

Cinnamon (7) and Cassia (8) Shavings of bark from the cinnamon tree are processed and curled to form cinnamon sticks. Also available in ground form. Spicy, fragrant and sweet, it is used widely in savoury and sweet dishes. Cassia (from the dried bark of the cassia tree) is similar, but less delicate in flavour.

Cloves (9) These dried, unopened flower buds give a warm aroma and pungency to foods, but should be used with care as the flavour can become overpowering. Whole cloves are added to hams, soups, sauces and mulled drinks as well as stewed fruits and apple pies. Also available in ground form for adding to cakes and puddings.

Coriander (10) Available in seed and ground form. These tiny, pale brown seeds have a mild, spicy flavour with a slight orange peel fragrance. An essential spice in curry dishes, but also extremely good in many cake and biscuit recipes.

Cumin (11) Sold in seed or ground form. Cumin has a warm, pungent aromatic flavour and is used extensively to flavour curries and many Middle Eastern and Mexican dishes. Popular in Germany for flavouring sauerkraut and port dishes. Use in meat stews and stuffed vegetables.

Fenugreek (12) These small, yellow-brown seeds have a slight bitter flavour which, when added in small quantities, is very good in curries, chutneys and pickles, soups and fish dishes.

Ginger (13) Available in many forms. Invaluable for adding to many savoury and sweet dishes and for baking traditional favourites such as gingerbread and brandy snaps. Fresh root ginger looks like a knobbly stem. It should be peeled and finely chopped or sliced before use. Dried ginger root is very hard and light beige in colour. To release flavour it should be 'bruised' with a spoon or soaked in hot water before using. This dried type is more often used in pickling, jam making and preserving. Also available in ground form, preserved stem ginger and crystallized ginger.

Mace (14) and Nutmeg (15) Both found on same plant. The nutmeg is the inner kernel of the fruit. When ripe, the fruit splits open to reveal bright red arils which lie around the shell of the nutmeg – and once dried are known as mace blades. The flavour of both spices is very similar – warm, sweet and aromatic, although nutmeg is more delicate than mace. Both spices are also sold ground. Use with vegetables; sprinkled over egg dishes, milk puddings and custards; egg nogs and mulled drinks; or use as a flavouring in cake mixtures.

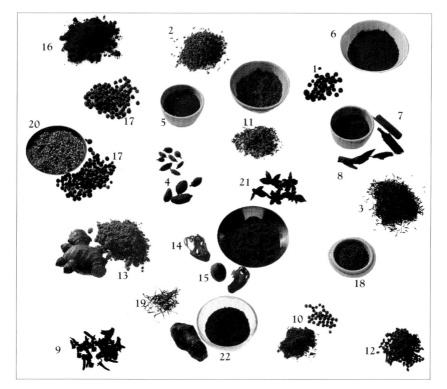

Paprika (16) Comes from a variety of pepper (capsicum) and although similar in colour to cayenne, this bright red powder has a mild flavour.

Pepper (17) White pepper comes from ripened berries with the outer husks removed. Black pepper comes from unripened berries dried until dark greenish black in colour. Black pepper is more subtle than white. Use white or black peppercorns in marinades and pickling, or freshly ground as a seasoning. Both white and black pepper are available ground. Green peppercorns are also unripe berries with a mild, light flavour. These are canned in brine or pickled, or freeze-dried in jars. They add a pleasant, light peppery flavour to sauces, pâtés and salad dressings. Drain those packed in liquid and use either whole or mash them lightly before using. Dry green peppercorns should be lightly crushed before using to help release flavour, unless otherwise stated in a recipe.

Poppy seeds (18) These tiny, slate-blue seeds add a nutty flavour to both sweet and savoury dishes.

Saffron (19) This spice comes from the stigmas of a species of crocus. It has a distinctive flavour and gives a rich

yellow colouring to dishes, however, it is also the most expensive spice. Available in small packets or jars (either powdered or in strands – the strands being far superior in flavour). This spice is a must for an authentic Paella or Cornish Saffron Cake. Also an extremely good flavouring for soups, fish and chicken dishes.

Sesame seeds (20) High in protein and mineral oil content, sesame seeds have a crisp texture and sweet, nutty flavour which combines well in curries, chicken, pork and fish dishes. Use to sprinkle over loaves, biscuits and pastries before baking.

Star Anise (21) This dried, star-shaped seed head has a pungent, aromatic smell, rather similar to fennel. Use very sparingly in stir-fry dishes; also good with fish and poultry.

Turmeric (22) Closely related to ginger, it is an aromatic root, which is dried and ground to produce a bright, orange/yellow powder. It has a rich, warm, distinctive smell and a delicate, aromatic flavour and helps give dishes an attractive yellow colouring. Use turmeric in curries; with fish and shellfish dishes; in rice pilaffs and lentil and other pulse mixtures.

SPICE MIXTURES

GARAM MASALA

10 green or 6 black cardamoms, pods cracked and seeds
  removed
1 tablespoon black peppercorns
2 teaspoons cumin seeds
½ teaspoon coriander seeds
2 small dried red chillies, seeds removed

Using a blender, grind all ingredients
together until finely ground. Store in an
airtight jar for up to 3 months. The amount of
spices used can be decreased or increased in
quantity, according to personal preference.

CURRY POWDER

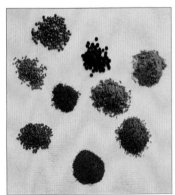

2 tablespoons cumin seeds
2 tablespoons fenugreek
1½ teaspoons mustard seeds
1 tablespoon black peppercorns
8 tablespoons coriander seeds
1 tablespoon poppy seeds
1 tablespoon ground ginger
1½ teaspoons hot chilli powder
4 tablespoons ground turmeric

Using a blender, grind first 6 ingredients
finely. Add remaining ingredients and grind.
Store in airtight jar for up to 3 months.

FIVE-SPICE POWDER

5 teaspoons ground anise (aniseed)
5 teaspoons star anise
12.5 cm (5 in) cinnamon stick, or use the equivalent
  in cassia bark
6 teaspoons cloves
7 teaspoons fennel seeds

Using a blender, grind all ingredients
together until finely ground. Store in an
airtight jar for up to 3 months. This is a
favourite for Chinese dishes. It is strong-
flavoured, so should only be used in very
small quantities.

MIXED SPICE

1 cinnamon stick, broken into small pieces
2½ teaspoons allspice berries
3 teaspoons cloves
2 teaspoons freshly grated nutmeg
3 teaspoons ground ginger

Using a coffee grinder, or blender, grind
cinnamon, allspice berries and cloves
together until very finely ground. Add to
freshly grated nutmeg and ginger and mix
well. Store in a small, airtight jar for up to 1
month.

PICKLING SPICE

2 tablespoons mace blades
1 tablespoon allspice berries
1 tablespoon whole cloves
2 cinnamon sticks, broken into small pieces
12 black peppercorns
1 dried bay leaf, crumbled

Mix all ingredients together. Store in a small,
airtight jar for up to 2 months.

HARISSA

30 g (1 oz) dried red chillies
1 clove garlic, chopped
1 teaspoon caraway seeds
1 teaspoon cumin seeds
1 teaspoon coriander seeds
several pinches of salt
olive oil, to cover

Soak chillies in hot water for 1 hour. Drain
well. Pat dry and, using a pestle and mortar,
grind to a smooth paste with garlic, spices and
salt. Put into a small jar, add enough olive oil
to cover. Store, covered, for up to 2 months.

MARINATED OLIVES

125 g (4 oz/³⁄₄ cup) black olives
125 g (4 oz/³⁄₄ cup) pimento-stuffed olives
3 slices of lemon
3 dried red chillies
2 cloves garlic, crushed
1 teaspoon mustard seeds
1 teaspoon black peppercorns
3 allspice berries
about 315 ml (10 fl oz/1³⁄₄ cups) olive oil
lemon twists and sprigs of parsley, to garnish

Drain off any brine from olives. Put olives into a bowl.

Add lemon slices, chillies, garlic, mustard seeds, peppercorns and allspice berries. Stir in olive oil and mix well. Spoon mixture into a large jar (with a tight-fitting lid). Screw on lid tightly and turn jar over several times to ensure ingredients are well mixed.

Leave olives to marinate for at least 1 week before serving, turning jar several times a day. Serve as an appetiser with drinks, garnished with lemon twists and sprigs of parsley. (These olives can be kept for up to 6 months in a cool place.)

Serves 4-6.

Note: Use a mixture of corn oil and olive oil, for a more economical marinade. Add sprigs of dried herbs to the marinade, if desired.

MUSHROOM CANAPÉS

30 g (1 oz/6 teaspoons) butter
125 g (4 oz) mushrooms, coarsely chopped
4 teaspoons plain flour
250 g (8 oz/2 cups) grated Cheddar cheese
1 teaspoon prepared mustard
1 teaspoon Worcestershire sauce
pepper
8 slices French bread, about 2 cm (¾ in) thick
1-2 tablespoons chopped fresh parsley
paprika for sprinkling
sprig of parsley, to garnish

Melt butter in a saucepan, add mushrooms and cook gently for 2 minutes. Stir flour into pan.

Add cheese, mustard and Worcestershire sauce. Stir well and heat through gently for 2 minutes until mixture begins to melt. Remove from heat and season to taste with pepper.

Toast slices of French bread on one side only. Spread cheese and mushroom mixture onto untoasted sides. Cook under a preheated hot grill for 3-4 minutes, or until melted and bubbling. Cut slices in half and sprinkle liberally with chopped parsley and paprika. Serve hot, garnished with parsley.

Serves 4.

BOMBAY NUT MIX

30 g (1 oz/²⁄₃ cup) thin pretzel sticks
45 g (1½ oz/9 teaspoons) butter
1 clove garlic, crushed
60 g (2 oz/⅓ cup) unblanched almonds
60 g (2 oz/⅓ cup) pine nuts
60 g (2 oz/⅓ cup) unsalted cashews
1 teaspoon Worcestershire sauce
1 teaspoon Curry Powder, see page 12
½ teaspoon hot chilli powder
60 g (2 oz/⅓ cup) seedless raisins
¼ teaspoon salt

Break pretzels into 2.5 cm (1 in) sticks. Melt butter in a frying pan.

Add garlic to pan, then stir in almonds, pine nuts and cashews. Add Worcestershire sauce, curry powder and chilli powder and mix well. Stir in pretzels and cook gently over medium heat for 3-4 minutes, stirring frequently.

Remove pan from heat. Add raisins and salt and mix well. Turn mixture into a serving dish and leave to cool.

Serves 4-6.

COCKTAIL KEBABS

8 large cooked prawns, thawed if frozen
2 spring onions, cut into short tassels
½ red pepper (capsicum), seeded and cut into
    shapes
8 small black or green olives
1 clove garlic, crushed
2 tablespoons lemon juice
2 tablespoons olive oil
1 teaspoon caster sugar
1 teaspoon wholegrain mustard
¼ teaspoon creamed horseradish

Remove heads and body shells from prawns but leave on tail shells.

De-vein prawns by removing the black spinal cord. Cut each spring onion into 4 pieces. Put prawns, onions, red pepper (capsicum) and olives into a bowl. Mix the garlic with the lemon juice, olive oil, sugar, mustard and horseradish in a small jug, stirring well together.

Pour mixture over ingredients in bowl, then cover and marinate for at least 2 hours, stirring occasionally. Lift ingredients out of marinade and thread equally onto 8 cocktail sticks. Allow to drain on absorbent kitchen paper before serving.

Makes 8.

Variation: Add small slices avocado to ingredients, if desired, and marinate and serve in the same way.

FILO PRAWN PARCELS

1 tablespoon sesame oil
2 tablespoons corn oil
1 clove garlic, crushed
1 onion, finely chopped
2.5 cm (1 in) fresh root ginger, peeled and grated
1/2 teaspoon turmeric
1/2 teaspoon chilli powder
1/4 teaspoon ground cumin
185 g (6 oz) peeled raw prawns, thawed if frozen
30 g (1 oz/2 tablespoons) creamed coconut, diced
5 sheets filo pastry
60 g (2 oz/1/4 cup) butter or ghee, melted
sprig of parsley, to garnish

Preheat oven to 180C (350F/Gas 4). Lightly grease a baking sheet. Heat sesame and corn oils in a saucepan. Add garlic, onion and ginger and fry gently for 5 minutes, stirring occasionally.

Add turmeric, chilli powder and cumin and fry gently for 2 minutes. Add prawns, then cover and cook gently for 5 minutes, stirring frequently. Remove from heat and stir in creamed coconut. Leave mixture to cool.

Work with 1-2 sheets of filo pastry at a time, keeping the rest covered with a damp cloth. Cut sheet of pastry in half lengthwise and then fold each piece in half lengthwise to give 2 long, narrow strips. Put a portion of prawn mixture in one corner of each strip of pastry. Brush pastry all over with a little of the melted butter or ghee.

Fold pastry and filling over at right angles to make a triangle and continue folding in this way along strip of pastry to form a neat triangular parcel. Brush all over with melted butter or ghee and put on greased baking sheet. Repeat this process with remaining sheets of pastry and prawn mixture, to make 10 parcels altogether.

Bake in oven for 20 minutes, then brush with remaining melted butter or ghee and return to oven for a further 5-10 minutes until parcels are golden brown. Serve warm, garnished with a sprig of parsley.

Makes 10.

TANGY POTTED CHEESE

125 g (4 oz/1 cup) finely grated mature Cheddar cheese
60 g (2 oz/¼ cup) butter, softened
3 teaspoons port or sherry
4 spring onions, finely chopped
½ teaspoon caraway seeds
½-1 teaspoon wholegrain mustard
¼ teaspoon Worcestershire sauce
30 g (1 oz/¼ cup) coarsely chopped walnuts
sprig of parsley, to garnish

Put grated cheese into a bowl and add softened butter. Mix well together until soft.

Stir in port or sherry, spring onions, caraway seeds, mustard and Worcestershire sauce and mix thoroughly until well combined.

Spoon mixture into a small dish, cover with chopped walnuts and press down lightly. Chill for at least 2 hours. Serve, garnished with parsley, with crackers or Melba toast.

Serves 4-6.

Note: This spread will keep in the refrigerator for up to 5 days.

Variation: Add 1 teaspoon chopped fresh herbs and a few pinches cayenne pepper to taste.

PIQUANT POPCORN

2 tablespoons corn oil
2 cloves garlic, crushed
1 cm (½ in) piece fresh root ginger, peeled and chopped
125 g (4 oz) popping corn
60 g (2 oz/¼ cup) butter
2 teaspoons hot chilli sauce
2 tablespoons chopped fresh parsley
salt

Heat oil in a large saucepan. Add 1 clove crushed garlic, the ginger and corn. Stir well.

Cover and cook over fairly high heat for 3-5 minutes, holding lid firmly and shaking pan frequently until popping stops. Turn popped corn into a dish, discarding any unpopped corn kernels. Melt butter in pan, add remaining crushed garlic clove and chilli sauce.

Return corn to pan and toss well until evenly coated with mixture. Add parsley and salt to taste and stir well. Turn into a serving dish. Serve warm or cold.

Serves 6-8.

Variation: Omit chilli sauce and instead add to melted butter: 1 teaspoon dry mustard, 1 teaspoon paprika, ½ teaspoon ground coriander and 2 tablespoons chopped fresh chives.

CHEESE CHILLI BITES

125 g (4 oz/1 cup) plain flour
¼ teaspoon salt
½ teaspoon dry mustard
¼-½ teaspoon hot chilli powder
large pinch of cayenne pepper
60g (2 oz/¼ cup) butter or margarine
60g (2 oz/½ cup) finely grated Cheddar cheese
1 egg, beaten
2 tablespoons sesame or poppy seeds

Preheat oven to 200C (400F/Gas 6). Sift flour, salt and spices into a bowl.

Rub in butter or margarine finely until mixture resembles breadcrumbs. Add grated cheese and mix well. Mix beaten egg with 1 tablespoon cold water. Add 2 tablespoons of egg mixture to bowl and mix to form a fairly stiff dough. Knead gently. Roll out dough on a lightly floured surface to a 15 x 30 cm (6 x 12 in) rectangle. Trim edges. Cut in half lengthwise and transfer to a baking sheet.

Brush each piece with remaining egg mixture and sprinkle with sesame or poppy seeds. Cut each piece into 10 triangular shapes and separate slightly to prevent them sticking together. Bake in oven for 10-12 minutes until lightly golden and cooked through. Cool on a wire rack.

Makes 20.

Note: Biscuits can be stored in an airtight container for up to 2 weeks.

MOZZARELLA SALAD

185 g (6 oz) Mozzarella cheese
2 large beefsteak tomatoes
2 ripe avocados
2 shallots
90 ml (3 fl oz/⅓ cup) olive oil
2 tablespoons lemon juice
½ teaspoon caster sugar
¼-½ teaspoon dry mustard
1-2 teaspoons green peppercorns, crushed
½ teaspoon dried oregano
salt
sprig of basil, to garnish
crusty bread or bread sticks, to serve

Thinly slice Mozzarella cheese and tomatoes
and arrange on 4 small plates.

Cut avocados in half, remove stones and
peel. Cut avocados into neat slices and
arrange on plate. Peel and thinly slice
shallots, separate into rings and scatter over
salad.

Put remaining ingredients, except basil and
bread, into a screw-topped jar, adding salt to
taste, and shake vigorously until well
blended. Spoon over salad and leave to
marinate for 1 hour before serving. Serve
chilled, garnished with basil, with warm
crusty bread or bread sticks.

Serves 4.

CHICKEN LIVER PÂTÉ

60g (2 oz/³⁄₄ cup) butter
1 onion, finely chopped
1 clove garlic, crushed
250 g (8 oz) chicken livers
1-2 teaspoons Curry Powder, see page 12
125 ml (4 fl oz/¹⁄₂ cup) chicken stock
2 hard-boiled eggs
salt and pepper
2 pinches of cayenne pepper
fresh bay leaves and lemon slices, to garnish

Melt half the butter in a frying pan. Add onion, garlic and chicken livers and cook gently for 5 minutes, stirring.

Add curry powder and cook for 1 minute, then add chicken stock and cook gently for 5 minutes, stirring and turning livers frequently. Put chicken liver mixture and hard-boiled eggs in a blender or food processor and blend to form a smooth purée.

Season with salt, pepper and cayenne pepper, then turn mixture into a small serving dish or terrine. Smooth the surface. Melt remaining butter in a pan and pour over surface of pâté. Leave to set slightly, then garnish with fresh bay leaves. Chill for several hours or overnight before adding lemon slices and serving with crusty bread.

Serves 6.

Note: Add a little curry powder to taste, to the melted butter topping, if desired.

MUSSEL SOUP

1 kg (2 lb) mussels
315 ml (10 fl oz/1¼ cups) dry white wine
45 g (1½ oz/9 teaspoons) butter
1 tablespoon olive oil
1 onion, finely chopped
1 clove garlic, crushed
1 leek, trimmed and finely shredded
½ teaspoon fenugreek, finely crushed
1½ tablespoons plain flour
315 ml (10 fl oz/1¼ cups) chicken stock
two 0.05 g packets saffron strands, soaked
   in 1 tablespoon boiling water
1 tablespoon chopped fresh parsley
salt and pepper
2 tablespoons whipping cream
sprig of parsley, to garnish

Scrub mussels clean in several changes of fresh cold water and pull off beards. Discard any mussels that are cracked or do not close tightly when tapped. Put mussels into a large saucepan with wine and 375 ml (12 fl oz/1½ cups) water. Cover and cook over high heat, shaking pan frequently, for 6-7 minutes or until shells open. Remove mussels from liquor, discarding any which remain closed. Strain liquid through a fine sieve and reserve.

Heat butter and oil in a pan. Add onion, garlic, leek and fenugreek and cook gently for 5 minutes. Stir in flour and cook for 1 minute, then add 625 ml (20 fl oz/2½ cups) reserved cooking liquor, chicken stock and saffron mixture. Bring to boil, cover and simmer for 15 minutes. Meanwhile, keep 8 mussels in shells and remove remaining mussels from shells. Add all mussels to soup and stir in parsley, seasoning and cream. Heat for 2-3 minutes. Garnish with parsley and serve.

Serves 4.

CHILLIED RED BEAN DIP

2 tablespoons corn oil
1 clove garlic, crushed
1 onion, finely chopped
1 fresh green chilli, seeded and finely chopped
1 teaspoon hot chilli powder
470 g (15 oz) can red kidney beans
60 g (2 oz/½ cup) grated mature Cheddar cheese
salt
thin slivers of fresh green and red chilli and sprig of
    parsley, to garnish
tortilla chips, to serve

Heat oil in a frying pan. Add garlic, onion, green chilli and chilli powder and cook gently for 4 minutes.

Drain kidney beans, reserving liquor. Reserve 3 tablespoons beans; purée the remainder in a blender or food processor. Add to pan and stir in 2 tablespoons reserved liquor and mix well.

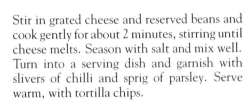

Stir in grated cheese and reserved beans and cook gently for about 2 minutes, stirring until cheese melts. Season with salt and mix well. Turn into a serving dish and garnish with slivers of chilli and sprig of parsley. Serve warm, with tortilla chips.

Serves 4-6.

Note: If mixture becomes too thick, add a little more bean liquid.

SPICED MELON COCKTAIL

½ ripe Honeydew melon, seeded
155 ml (5 fl oz/⅔ cup) whipping cream
155 ml (5 fl oz/⅔ cup) mayonnaise
2 teaspoons lemon juice
1 teaspoon paprika
½ teaspoon Tabasco sauce
½ teaspoon Worcestershire sauce
2 tablespoons tomato purée (paste)
250 g (8 oz) white crabmeat, flaked
8 radicchio leaves, shredded
lemon and lime slices and sprig of mint, to garnish

Cut melon flesh into neat pieces, or scoop melon into balls, see Note.

In a bowl, whip cream until softly peaking. Mix in mayonnaise, lemon juice, paprika, Tabasco sauce, Worcestershire sauce and tomato purée (paste).

Stir crabmeat into dressing, then lightly mix in melon and toss ingredients gently until coated. Arrange shredded radicchio in 4 individual serving dishes and spoon the melon and crab mixture on top. Serve lightly chilled, garnished with lemon and lime slices and mint.

Serves 4.

Note: For melon balls, use a melon scoop and 1 ripe Honeydew melon (use left-over melon in a fruit salad).

VEGETABLE SAMOSAS

250 g (8 oz) potatoes, cut in even-sized pieces
125 g (4 oz) frozen peas
2 tablespoons corn oil
1 onion, finely chopped
½ teaspoon cumin seeds
1 cm (½ in) piece fresh root ginger, peeled and grated
½ teaspoon turmeric
½ teaspoon Garam Masala, see page 12
½ teaspoon salt
2 teaspoons lemon juice
125 g (4 oz/1 cup) plain flour
30 g (1 oz/6 teaspoons) butter
2 tablespoons warm milk
vegetable oil for deep frying
Mango chutney, to serve, see page 89
celery leaves and lime twists, to garnish

Boil potatoes in salted water for 15-20 minutes until tender. Drain well, return to saucepan and shake over a low heat for a few moments to dry off. Mash well. Cook peas in boiling, salted water for 4 minutes. Drain well.

Heat corn oil in a frying pan. Add onion, cumin seeds, ginger, turmeric, garam masala and salt and cook gently for 5 minutes. Add mashed potato and peas, then stir in lemon juice. Mix well together and remove from heat and cool.

Sift flour into a bowl. Rub in butter finely until mixture resembles breadcrumbs. Add milk and mix to form a stiff dough. Divide into 6 equal portions.

Form each piece into a ball, then roll out on a lightly floured work surface to form 15 cm (6 in) rounds. Cut each round in half. Divide filling equally between semi-circles of pastry.

Dampen edges of pastry then fold over and seal to form triangular-shaped pasties which enclose the filling completely. Half-fill a deep fat pan or fryer with oil; heat to 190C (375F) or until a cube of day-old bread browns in 40 seconds. Fry samosas, a few at a time, in hot oil for 3-4 minutes until golden. Drain on absorbent kitchen paper. Serve hot. garnished with celery leaves and lime twists, with mango chutney.

Makes 12.

AUBERGINE TAHINI PÂTÉ

1 large aubergine (eggplant)
1 large clove garlic
3 shallots
½-1 teaspoon Garam Masala, see page 12
3 tablespoons tahini (creamed sesame)
finely grated peel of 1 lemon
3 tablespoons lemon juice
salt
2 teaspoons olive oil
cayenne pepper for sprinkling
lemon slices and sprig of parsley, to garnish
pitta bread, to serve

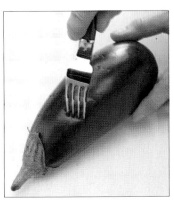

Preheat oven to 180C (350F/Gas 4). Prick aubergine (eggplant) with a fork.

Bake aubergine (eggplant) in the oven for 30-40 minutes until softened and skin has turned dark brown. Trim ends and peel. Purée flesh in a blender or food processor with garlic, shallots, garam masala, tahini, lemon peel and juice until smooth and evenly combined.

Add salt to taste. Turn mixture into a serving bowl, drizzle with olive oil and sprinkle with cayenne pepper. Garnish with lemon slices and sprig of parsley. Serve with warm fingers of pitta bread.

Serves 4-6.

– ONION & MUSHROOM BHAJIS –

1 onion
60 g (2 oz) button mushrooms
45 g (1½ oz/⅓ cup) brown rice flour
45 g (1½ oz/⅓ cup) plain flour
½ teaspoon turmeric
½ teaspoon hot chilli powder
¼ teaspoon ground cumin
¼ teaspoon ground coriander
¼ teaspoon salt
155 ml (5 fl oz/⅔ cup) natural yogurt
vegetable oil for deep frying
sprig of parsley, to garnish

Peel, quarter and thinly slice onion.

Coarsely chop mushrooms. Put brown rice flour and plain flour in a bowl. Add turmeric, chilli powder, cumin, coriander and salt. Stir in yogurt, onion and mushrooms. Mix well.

Half-fill a deep fat pan or fryer with oil and heat to 190C (375F) or until a cube of day-old bread browns in 40 seconds. Divide mixture into 10 equal portions. Drop spoonfuls of mixture into hot oil and fry for 3-4 minutes until golden brown and cooked through. Drain on absorbent kitchen paper. Serve warm, garnished with a sprig of parsley.

Makes 10.

DEVILLED TOMATOES

4 firm tomatoes
30 g (1 oz/6 teaspoons) butter
1 small clove garlic, crushed
30 g (1 oz/½ cup) fresh white breadcrumbs
1 tablespoon chopped fresh parsley
¼ teaspoon cayenne pepper
½ teaspoon paprika
½ teaspoon dry mustard
3 teaspoons grated Parmesan cheese
salt
sprigs of parsley, to garnish

Preheat oven to 180C (350F/Gas 4). Grease
an ovenproof dish. Cut the top one-third off
each tomato.

Reserve tops for 'lids'. Scoop out some of the
seeds from each tomato. Arrange tomatoes,
cut-sides up, in the dish. Melt butter in a
saucepan. Add garlic, breadcrumbs and
parsley and mix well together.

Remove from heat and add cayenne pepper,
paprika, mustard and Parmesan cheese.
Season with salt and mix well. Spoon onto
tomatoes and form into neat mounds,
pressing gently into shape with fingertips. Put
reserved 'lids' on top. Bake in oven for 15
minutes. Serve hot, garnished with sprigs of
parsley.

Serves 4.

ORIENTAL PRAWNS

8 raw Mediterranean (king) prawns
60 g (2 oz/½ cup) plain flour
¼ teaspoon salt
1 teaspoon corn oil
2.5 cm (1 in) piece fresh root ginger, peeled and grated
1 clove garlic, crushed
1 teaspoon chilli sauce
1 egg white
vegetable oil for frying
spring onion tassel and few strips of red pepper, to
    garnish

Peel prawns, leaving tail shells on. Make a small incision along the spines. Remove black spinal cords from prawns.

Put flour into a bowl. Add salt, oil and 60 ml (2 fl oz/¼ cup) water and mix together. Stir in ginger, garlic and chilli sauce and beat well. In a bowl, whisk egg white until stiff, then gently fold into batter until evenly combined.

Half-fill a deep fat pan or fryer with oil and heat to 190C (375F) or until a cube of day-old bread browns in 40 seconds. Hold each prawn by its tail and dip it into batter, then lower it into hot oil. Fry for 3 minutes until golden. Drain on absorbent kitchen paper. Serve hot, garnished with spring onion tassel and red pepper strips.

Serves 4.

CREOLE GUMBO POT

1 small aubergine (eggplant)
salt and pepper
3 tablespoons olive oil
1 large onion, chopped
1 red pepper (capsicum), seeded and diced
1 clove garlic, crushed
2 teaspoons paprika
1/2 teaspoon hot chilli powder
125 g (4 oz) okra
125 g (4 oz) frozen sweetcorn, thawed
470 ml (15 fl oz/2 cups) boiling chicken stock
250 g (8 oz) can tomatoes
30 g (1 oz/2 tablespoons) long-grain rice
250 g (8 oz) peeled prawns, thawed if frozen
sprig of dill, to garnish

Trim stalk end from aubergine (eggplant). Cut aubergine (eggplant) into 1 cm (1/2 in) pieces and put into a colander. Sprinkle with 2 teaspoons salt and leave on a plate to drain for 30 minutes. Rinse under cold water and drain well.

Heat oil in a saucepan. Add onion, red pepper (capsicum), garlic and aubergine (eggplant) and fry gently over low heat for 5 minutes, stirring frequently.

Stir in paprika and chilli powder and cook gently for 2 minutes. Trim stalk ends from okra and discard. Cut okra into quarters.

Add okra to pan together with sweetcorn, boiling chicken stock and the tomatoes. Break tomatoes up with a spoon. Stir in rice, then cover and simmer gently for 25 minutes until vegetables and rice are tender.

Add prawns to the mixture and heat through for 5 minutes, stirring occasionally. Taste and adjust seasoning if necessary with salt and pepper. Serve hot, garnished with dill.

Serves 4-6.

Variation: For a deliciously rich version, stir in 155 ml (5 fl oz/⅔ cup) single (light) cream just before serving and heat through gently.

DHAL

250 g (8 oz/1¼ cups) brown lentils
1 teaspoon turmeric
1 clove garlic, crushed
30 g (1 oz/6 teaspoons) ghee
1 large onion, chopped
1 teaspoon Garam Masala, see page 12
½ teaspoon ground ginger
1 teaspoon ground coriander
½ teaspoon cayenne pepper
coriander leaves, to garnish

Wash lentils in cold water.

Place lentils in a saucepan with 940 ml (30 fl oz/3¾ cups) water, turmeric and garlic. Stir well, then cover and simmer for 30 minutes until tender. Uncover and cook for 2-3 minutes to reduce excess liquid.

Heat ghee in a pan. Add onion and fry gently for 5 minutes, then add garam masala, ginger, coriander and cayenne and cook gently for 1 minute. Add mixture to lentils and stir well. Serve hot, garnished with coriander leaves.

Serves 4-6.

Note: for a less fiery flavour, reduce cayenne pepper.

BARBECUED SPARE RIBS

1 kg (2lb) pork spare ribs (sheets)
2 tablespoons dark soy sauce
1 tablespoon tomato purée (paste)
2 good pinches of Five-Spice Powder, see page 12
3 tablespoons clear honey
1 clove garlic, crushed
1 cm (½ in) piece fresh root ginger, peeled and grated
125 ml (4 fl oz/½ cup) unsweetened orange juice
¼ teaspoon prepared mustard
slices of orange peel, to garnish

Preheat oven to 190C (375F/Gas 5). Cut ribs into single portion ribs and arrange in a single layer in a large roasting dish.

Mix the remaining ingredients together in a bowl until thoroughly combined. Spoon approximately half quantity over ribs and bake in oven for 30 minutes.

Increase oven temperature to 200C (400F/Gas 6). Turn ribs and spoon over the remaining sauce. Bake for a further 50-60 minutes, basting and turning frequently until ribs are glazed and rich golden brown. Serve hot, garnished with slices of orange peel.

Serves 4.

FRIED CAMEMBERT

four 45 g (1½ oz) portions fairly firm Camembert
2 teaspoons plain flour
½ teaspoon dry mustard
½ teaspoon dried mixed herbs
pepper
1 egg, beaten
30 g (1 oz/¼ cup) golden breadcrumbs
½ teaspoon hot chilli powder
3-4 pinches of cayenne pepper
vegetable oil for deep frying
sprigs of rosemary, sage and thyme, to garnish

Wrap and freeze portions of Camembert for 1 hour.

On a plate, mix together the flour, mustard, herbs and season with pepper. Rub each portion of cheese thoroughly with the mixture, then dip into beaten egg. Mix breadcrumbs with chilli powder and cayenne pepper. Coat dipped cheese portions in mixture, pressing on firmly with palms of hands.

Half-fill a deep fat pan or fryer with oil and heat to 190C (375F) or until a cube of day-old bread browns in 40 seconds. Fry portions of cheese for about 30 seconds until golden brown. Drain on absorbent kitchen paper and serve at once, garnished with sprigs of rosemary, sage and thyme.

Serves 4.

GUACAMOLE

2 ripe avocados
1 tablespoon lemon juice
1 small clove garlic, if desired
1 small fresh green chilli, seeded
1 shallot, finely chopped
1 tablespoon olive oil
few drops Tabasco sauce
salt
slices of lemon and sprig of parsley, to garnish
tortilla chips, to serve

Cut avocados in half, remove stones and scoop flesh onto a plate. Mash well.

Add lemon juice and garlic, if desired, and mix well. Very finely chop chilli and add to mixture together with chopped shallot.

Stir in oil, Tabasco sauce and salt and mix well together. Turn mixture into a serving bowl, garnish with slices of lemon and sprig of parsley and serve with tortilla chips.

Serves 4-6.

EGG INDIENNE

4 hard-boiled eggs
100 g (3½ oz) can tuna, drained and flaked
125 ml (4 fl oz/½ cup) mayonnaise
salt and pepper
4 cocktail gherkins, chopped
8 small lettuce leaves for serving
3 tablespoons single (light) cream
2 teaspoons tomato purée (paste)
1½ teaspoons Curry Powder, see page 12
paprika for sprinkling
sprigs of chervil, to garnish

Cut eggs in half lengthwise and carefully remove yolks.

Put yolks into a bowl. Add tuna, 2 tablespoons mayonnaise, seasoning and chopped gherkins and mix well together. Divide mixture evenly between egg whites and use to fill hollows. Smooth over tops to form neat mounds and arrange on a bed of lettuce leaves on a serving dish.

In a bowl, mix together the remaining mayonnaise with cream, tomato purée (paste) and curry powder and season with salt. Mix well until smooth. Spoon mixture over prepared eggs to coat completely. Sprinkle with paprika and garnish with sprigs of chervil. Serve chilled.

Serves 4.

DEVILLED WHITEBAIT

375 g (12 oz) whitebait, thawed if frozen
30 g (1 oz/¼ cup) plain flour
¼ teaspoon salt
1 teaspoon dry mustard
¼ teaspoon cayenne pepper
½ teaspoon paprika
finely grated peel of 1 lemon
vegetable oil for frying
1-2 tablespoons chopped fresh parsley, lemon peel
  and sprigs of dill, to garnish
lemon wedges, to serve

Rinse whitebait under cold running water. Pat dry on absorbent kitchen paper.

Mix together the flour, salt, mustard, cayenne pepper, paprika and lemon peel in a polythene bag. Add whitebait and shake well until fish are evenly coated. Half-fill a deep fat pan or fryer with oil and heat to 190C (375F) or until a cube of day-old bread browns in 40 seconds. Place half whitebait in frying basket and lower gradually into hot oil and fry for 1 minute only, shaking basket frequently. Drain on absorbent kitchen paper.

Repeat with remaining whitebait. Reheat oil to same temperature. Place whole quantity whitebait into basket and fry for 1-2 minutes until lightly golden and crisp. Drain on absorbent kitchen paper. Turn into a warmed serving dish and garnish with chopped parsley, lemon peel and sprigs of dill. Serve hot with lemon wedges.

Serves 4.

SESAME PRAWN TOASTS

185 g (6 oz) peeled prawns, thawed if frozen
2 cm (³⁄₄ in) piece fresh root ginger, peeled and grated
1 clove garlic, crushed
2 teaspoons cornflour
1 egg white
3 pinches of Five-Spice Powder, see page 12
salt and pepper
4 thin slices white bread, crusts removed
3 tablespoons sesame seeds
vegetable oil for shallow frying
spring onion flowers, to garnish

Drain prawns thoroughly on absorbent kitchen paper.

Mince prawns finely and mix with ginger, garlic and cornflour. In a bowl, lightly whisk egg white with a fork (just enough to make frothy) and add to mixture. Stir in five-spice powder and seasoning and mix well together.

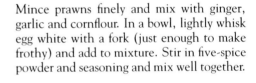

Press prawn mixture evenly and firmly onto slices of bread. Sprinkle with sesame seeds and press on firmly. Heat 2 cm (³⁄₄ in) oil in a large frying pan. Lower slices, prawn-sides down, into hot oil and fry for 2-3 minutes until golden brown. Keep slices immersed in oil all the time, by pressing with a fish slice. Drain on absorbent kitchen paper. Cut into fingers and serve hot, garnished with spring onion flowers.

Serves 4.

MULLIGATAWNY SOUP

30 g (1 oz/6 teaspoons) butter
1 tablespoon corn oil
1 large onion, chopped
2 celery sticks, sliced thinly
3 carrots, diced
4 teaspoons Curry Powder, see page 12
6 teaspoons plain flour
1.2 litres (40 fl oz/5 cups) chicken stock
30 g (1 oz/2 tablespoons) long-grain rice
2 tomatoes, skinned and chopped
250 g (8 oz) cooked chicken, diced
1 small cooking apple, peeled, cored and diced
salt
carrot twist and celery leaves, to garnish

Heat butter and oil in a saucepan

Add onion, celery and carrots and cook gently for 5 minutes. Stir in curry powder and flour and cook for 1 minute. Stir in stock and bring to the boil, then add rice and stir well.

Cover and simmer for 20 minutes, stirring occasionally. Add tomatoes, chicken and apple. Season with salt, then cover again and simmer for 15 minutes. Serve hot, garnished with a carrot twist and celery leaves.

Serves 4.

BEEF SATAY

3 tablespoons corn oil
1 small onion, finely chopped
1 clove garlic, crushed
½ teaspoon hot chilli powder
1-1½ teaspoons Curry Powder, see page 12
185 g (6 oz) crunchy peanut butter
1 teaspoon light soft brown sugar
2 teaspoons dark soy sauce
1 teaspoon lemon juice
salt and pepper
500 g (1 lb) rump steak
lemon slices and coriander leaves, to garnish

Heat 2 tablespoons oil in a saucepan. Add onion and garlic and fry gently until golden.

Add chilli powder, curry powder, 315 ml (10 fl oz/1¼ cups) water, peanut butter and sugar and bring to the boil. Simmer gently until thickened. Stir in soy sauce and lemon juice, then season with salt and pepper. Turn mixure into a serving dish.

Cut meat into 1 cm (½ in) cubes. Thread (not too tightly) onto 8 bamboo skewers, leaving a space at each end for holding. Cover ends with small pieces of foil. Place skewers in a greased grill pan. Brush with reserved 1 tablespoon oil. Cook under a hot grill for 10-15 minutes until golden and cooked through. Turn and brush frequently with oil during cooking. Serve hot, garnished with lemon slices and coriander leaves, with the peanut sauce.

Serves 4.

PIQUANT SALMON ROLLS

60 g (2 oz) cream cheese
30 g (1 oz/¼ cup) walnuts, chopped
1 tablespoon chopped fresh chives
1 stick celery, chopped
2 teaspoons lemon juice
several pinches of cayenne pepper
¼ teaspoon ground coriander
8 thin slices of smoked salmon, about 5 cm (2 in) wide
    and 10 cm (4 in) long
8 thin slices brown bread
a little butter for spreading
8 thin slices of cucumber
freshly ground black pepper
sprigs of dill and chives, to garnish

In a bowl, soften cream cheese.

Stir walnuts, chives and celery into cheese. Add 1 teaspoon lemon juice and spices and mix well, then divide equally into 8 and spread each portion on a slice of salmon and roll up to form neat rolls.

Toast bread and cut out eight 6 cm (2½ in) rounds, using a biscuit cutter. Spread thinly with butter. Arrange a cucumber slice on each one and put a salmon roll on top. Drizzle with remaining lemon juice and sprinkle with pepper. Garnish with dill and chives.

Serves 4.

Note: The salmon rolls can be prepared several hours in advance and kept chilled. The toast bases however, are nicer eaten freshly made.

BEEF LETTUCE CUPS

375 g (12 oz) rump steak
2 tablespoons light soy sauce
1 tablespoon dry sherry
1 cm (½ in) piece fresh root ginger, peeled and grated
1 clove garlic, crushed
2 pinches of Five-Spice Powder, see page 12
1 teaspoon chilli sauce
2 tablespoons corn oil
6 spring onions, sliced diagonally
1 small red pepper (capsicum), seeded and diced
½ teaspoon cornflour
8 crisp lettuce cups, to serve
sprig of parsley, to garnish

Cut steak into thin slivers and put in a bowl.

Add soy sauce, sherry, ginger, garlic, five-spice powder and chilli sauce. Mix well, then cover and marinate in refrigerator for 1 hour, stirring occasionally. Heat oil in a large frying pan or wok. Add onions and red pepper (capsicum) and stir-fry for 1 minute.

Add beef mixture to pan and stir-fry for 2-3 minutes. Blend cornflour smoothly with 1 teaspoon water and add to pan. Cook for 1 minute, stirring all the time. Turn mixture into a warm serving dish. Serve at once with chilled lettuce cups, garnished with sprig of parsley.

Serves 4.

Note: To serve, simply spoon beef mixture into lettuce cups and eat with the fingers. Accompany this dish with finger bowls.

CURRY CREAM MUSSELS

1 kg (2 lb) mussels, cleaned, see page 25
155 ml (5 fl oz/¾ cup) dry cider
3 sprigs of thyme
1 clove garlic, crushed
30 g (1 oz/6 teaspoons) butter
3 shallots, finely chopped
1 stick celery, finely chopped
3 teaspoons Curry Powder, see page 12
3 teaspoons plain flour
60 ml (2 fl oz/¼ cup) single (light) cream
60 ml (2 fl oz/¼ cup) mayonnaise
sprigs of dill or parsley, to garnish
hot crusty bread, to serve

Place cleaned mussels in a large saucepan with 155 ml (5 fl oz/⅔ cup) water, cider, thyme and garlic. Cover and cook over high heat, shaking pan frequently, for 6-7 minutes, or until shells open. Discard any mussels which remain closed. Leave mussels to cool in liquor. Drain off cooled liquor, discarding thyme, then strain through a fine sieve and reserve. Remove a half shell from each mussel and arrange mussels on 4 serving plates.

Melt butter in a pan. Add shallots and celery and cook gently for 5 minutes. Add curry powder and flour and cook for 1 minute. Stir in 250 ml (8 fl oz/1 cup) reserved liquor and bring to the boil, stirring. Cover and cook gently for 10 minutes, stirring frequently. Cool. Stir in cream and mayonnaise and mix well. Spoon sauce over mussels and garnish with sprigs of dill or parsley. Serve with hot crusty bread.

Serves 4

GADO GADO

250 g (8 oz) white cabbage
60 ml (2 fl oz/¼ cup) sesame oil
1 large onion, quartered and thinly sliced
1 green pepper (capsicum), seeded and thinly sliced
185 g (6 oz) fresh beansprouts
1 fresh green chilli, seeded and finely chopped
1 clove garlic, crushed
2 shallots, finely chopped
½ teaspoon ground cumin
125 g (4 oz) smooth peanut butter
3 tablespoons lemon juice
few drops Tabasco sauce
red pepper (capsicum) strips, to garnish

Finely shred cabbage, discarding stalk.

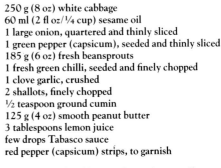

Heat 2 tablespoons oil in a large frying pan. Add shredded cabbage, onion, green pepper (capsicum), beansprouts and chilli and fry over fairly high heat for 3-4 minutes, stirring all the time. Remove from heat, turn mixture into a serving dish and leave to cool.

Heat remaining oil in a small pan. Add garlic, shallots and cumin and fry gently for 5 minutes. Add peanut butter and cook gently for 2 minutes. Stir in lemon juice, Tabasco sauce and 90 ml (3 fl oz/⅓ cup) water and heat through gently to form a fairly thick sauce. Serve warm, garnished with red pepper (capsicum) strips, with cooled vegetables.

Serves 4-6.

— PEPPERED FARMHOUSE PÂTÉ —

8 rashers smoked streaky bacon
500 g (1 lb) belly pork rashers
375 g (12 oz) pig's liver
1 onion, quartered
1 clove garlic
250 g (8 oz) veal escalope
1 egg, beaten
1 teaspoon salt
2 teaspoons green peppercorns
1 teaspoon dried mixed herbs
2 tablespoons brandy
green peppercorns and bay leaf, to garnish
crusty bread, to serve

Preheat oven to 180C (350F/Gas 4). Remove rinds and bones from bacon and pork.

Stretch bacon rashers on a board with the back of a knife until almost double in length. Use to line base and sides of a 1.2 litre (40 fl oz/5 cup) terrine or soufflé dish. Mince belly pork, liver, onion and garlic into a bowl. Cut veal into 1 cm (½ in) pieces and add to bowl. Stir in beaten egg, salt, peppercorns, herbs and brandy and mix thoroughly.

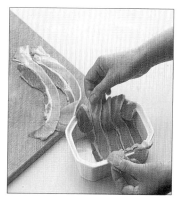

Spoon mixture into bacon-lined dish and smooth over surface. Cover tightly with foil. Put into a roasting tin, half-filled with hot water. Bake in oven for 2 hours. Cool for 30 minutes, then top with a plate and weight down with a heavy weight. Leave to cool completely, then refrigerate overnight. Turn out onto a serving plate. Serve, garnished with green peppercorns and a bay leaf, with crusty bread.

Serves 8.

— ORANGE GINGER DUCKLING —

2 kg (4 lb) oven-ready duckling
250 g (8 oz) mange tout (snow peas)
1 red pepper (capsicum), seeded
3 tablespoons corn oil
3 sticks celery, sliced diagonally
12 spring onions, sliced diagonally
7.5 cm (3 in) piece fresh root ginger, peeled and
   chopped
1 tablespoon granulated sugar
1 tablespoon soy sauce
1 tablespoon dry sherry
1 tablespoon malt vinegar
1 tablespoon tomato purée (paste)
2 teaspoons cornflour
155 ml (5 fl oz/²⁄₃ cup) orange juice
orange slices and mange tout (snow peas), to garnish

Preheat oven to 180C (350F/Gas 4). Prick duckling skin all over with a fork and put in a roasting tin. Bake in oven for 1¾ hours until golden and cooked. Top and tail mange tout (snow peas). Cut red pepper (capsicum) into small diamonds. Leave duck to cool, then strip flesh and skin from carcass. Cut into thin strips. Heat 2 tablespoons oil in a large frying pan. Add mange tout (snow peas) and celery and stir-fry for 2 minutes. Add spring onions, red pepper (capsicum) and ginger and stir-fry for 2 minutes. Remove from pan and keep warm.

Heat remaining oil in pan. Add duckling and stir-fry 2 minutes. Remove from pan. Mix sugar, soy sauce, sherry, vinegar and tomato purée (paste) in a bowl. Blend cornflour with a little orange juice. Add rest of juice. Add to bowl. Stir into pan. Bring to boil, stirring. Lower heat and simmer 2 minutes. Return vegetables and duckling to pan; heat. Serve, garnished with orange and mange tout.

Serves 4.

Note: Serve with rice and prawn crackers.

TROPICAL FISH KEBABS

1 kg (2 lb) monkfish
2 cloves garlic, crushed
1 fresh green chilli, seeded and chopped
2.5 cm (1 in) piece fresh root ginger, peeled and
  chopped
juice of 1 lime
75 ml (2½ fl oz/⅓ cup) corn oil
salt and pepper
1 ripe mango
2 bananas
1 red pepper (capsicum), seeded and cubed
rice salad, to serve
wedges of lime, to garnish

Cut away monkfish from central bone. Cut flesh into neat bite-sized pieces.

Mix together in a shallow glass dish, the garlic, chilli, ginger, lime juice and oil and season with salt and pepper. Add fish, stir gently, then cover and marinate in refrigerator for 2 hours. Meanwhile, prepare mango. Slice mango lengthwise on each side, close to the stone. Peel and cut mango flesh into neat pieces.

Cut bananas into chunky pieces. Thread pieces of fish onto 4 long (or 8 short) bamboo skewers, alternating fish with cubes of red pepper (capsicum), mango and banana. Arrange skewers in a grill pan and spoon over marinade. Cook under grill for 12-15 minutes, turning frequently and spooning with marinade, until cooked through. Serve hot with rice salad, garnished with wedges of lime.

Serves 4.

SPICED CHICKEN PILAU

60 g (2 oz/¼ cup) ghee
2 large onions, thinly sliced
4 boneless chicken breasts, cubed
½ teaspoon turmeric
375 g (12 oz/2 cups) basmati rice
940 ml (30 fl oz/3¾ cups) boiling chicken stock
5 green cardamom pods, crushed and seeds removed
½ teaspoon ground cinnamon
4 whole cloves
½ teaspoon fenugreek
1 teaspoon salt
125 g (4 oz) frozen peas, thawed
90 g (3oz/½ cup) unsalted cashews
90 g (3 oz/½ cup) sultanas
strips of red pepper (capsicum), spring onion and sprig
    of parsley, to garnish

Melt ghee in a large saucepan. Add onions
and chicken and fry for 3 minutes, stirring all
the time. Add turmeric and rice and cook for
2 minutes, stirring. Add boiling stock,
cardamom seeds, cinnamon, cloves,
fenugreek and salt and bring to the boil. Stir
well, then cover tightly and cook gently for
20 minutes.

Add peas, cashews and sultanas, fluff up
mixture with a fork, then cover and continue
cooking for a further 10 minutes. Fluff up
with a fork and serve hot, garnished with
strips of red pepper (capsicum) and spring
onion and sprig of parsley.

Serves 6.

—— PEPPERED SALAMI SALAD ——

8 tablespoons olive oil
2 cloves garlic, crushed
3 slices white bread, crusts removed and cubed
½ teaspoon chilli seasoning
250 g (8 oz) young spinach or 1 cos lettuce
185 g (6 oz) piece peppered salami, diced
3 small onions, sliced and separated into rings
1 red pepper (capsicum), seeded and cut into thin strips
125 g (4 oz) button mushrooms, sliced
1½ tablespoons lemon juice
1 teaspoon caster sugar
1 teaspoon prepared mustard
salt and pepper
12 Marinated Olives, see page 14

Heat 3 tablespoons oil in a frying pan. Add garlic and bread cubes and fry, stirring, until golden. Remove from heat, add chilli seasoning, stir well and cool. Tear spinach or lettuce leaves into bite-sized pieces and put into a bowl. Add salami, onion rings, red pepper (capsicum) and mushrooms.

Place remaining oil in a screw-top jar with lemon juice, sugar and mustard and season with salt and pepper. Shake vigorously until well blended. Spoon over ingredients in bowl and toss well together. Scatter bread croûtons on top and garnish with olives. Serve at once.

Serves 4.

Note: Salad (without dressing) may be prepared in advance and kept covered in refrigerator.

SINGAPORE PARCELS

125 g (4 oz/1 cup) plain flour
1 large egg
155 ml (5 fl oz/⅔ cup) milk
5 tablespoons corn oil
250 g (8 oz) lean minced beef
1 onion, chopped
2 carrots, grated
1 parsnip, grated
2 teaspoons Curry Powder, see page 12
3 teaspoons tomato purée (paste)
2 teaspoons cornflour
155 ml (5 fl oz/⅔ cup) beef stock
a little beaten egg for brushing
vegetable oil for deep frying
carrot strips, to garnish

Sift flour into a bowl. Make a well in centre and add egg. Gradually stir in milk and beat well until smooth. Stir in 155 ml (5 fl oz/⅔ cup) cold water and beat well. Pour batter into a jug.

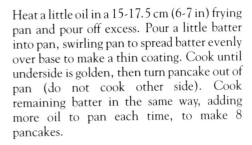

Heat a little oil in a 15-17.5 cm (6-7 in) frying pan and pour off excess. Pour a little batter into pan, swirling pan to spread batter evenly over base to make a thin coating. Cook until underside is golden, then turn pancake out of pan (do not cook other side). Cook remaining batter in the same way, adding more oil to pan each time, to make 8 pancakes.

Heat 3 tablespoons oil in a saucepan. Add minced beef, onion, carrots, parsnip and curry powder and cook gently for 5 minutes, stirring. Add tomato purée (paste) and mix well. Blend cornflour with a little stock. Add remaining stock to pan and bring to the boil. Add cornflour mixture and cook for 2 minutes, stirring all the time. Simmer mixture for 10 minutes. Leave until cold.

Put pancakes, cooked-sides up, on a work surface and spread filling in a 5 cm (2 in) horizontal line across centre to within 4 cm (1½ in) of side edges. Fold these side edges over mixture and then fold the remaining top and bottom edges over to cover filling. Brush with beaten egg. Chill for 1 hour.

Half-fill a deep fat pan or fryer with oil and heat to 190C (375F) or until a cube of day-old bread browns in 40 seconds. Fry parcels, 4 at a time, for 2-3 minutes until golden brown and heated through. Drain on absorbent kitchen paper and serve hot, garnished with carrot strips.

Serves 8.

DEVILLED CRAB QUICHE

250 g (8 oz/2 cups) plain flour
½ teaspoon salt
½ teaspoon chilli seasoning
60 g (2 oz/¼ cup) block margarine, diced
60 g (2 oz/¼ cup) lard, diced
60 g (2 oz/½ cup) finely grated Cheddar cheese
6 rashers streaky bacon, chopped
1 onion, chopped
125 g (4 oz) crabmeat, flaked
3 eggs
155 ml (5 fl oz/⅔ cup) single (light) cream
½ teaspoon dry mustard
¼ teaspoon cayenne pepper
tomato and sprig of parsley, to garnish

Preheat oven to 200C (400F/Gas 6).

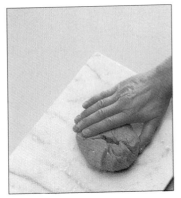

Put flour, salt and chilli seasoning into a bowl. Add margarine and lard and rub in finely until mixture resembles breadcrumbs. Add cheese and mix well. Stir in 3 tablespoons water and mix to form a firm dough. Knead gently. Roll out pastry and use to line a 25 cm (10 in) loose-bottomed, fluted flan tin, set on a baking sheet. Press pastry well into flutes and trim edge neatly. Prick base all over with a fork. Line flan with a piece of greaseproof paper and fill with baking beans.

Bake in the oven for 15 minutes, then remove paper and beans and return flan to oven for a further 5-10 minutes until dry and lightly golden. Meanwhile, dry-fry bacon in a pan for 3 minutes. Add onion and cook for 2 minutes. Remove from heat and mix with crabmeat. Spoon mixture into flan case. Whisk together eggs, cream, mustard and cayenne and season with salt. Pour into flan case. Bake for 30-35 minutes until golden. Serve, garnished with tomato and parsley.

Serves 6-8.

MUSTARD PORK

15 g (½ oz/3 teaspoons) butter
1 tablespoon vegetable oil
4 pork steaks, each weighing about 185 g (6 oz)
1 onion, finely chopped
1 clove garlic, crushed
1 tablespoon wholegrain or Dijon mustard
4 tablespoons dry white wine
3 tablespoons single (light) cream
salt and pepper
155 g (5 oz) Mozzarella cheese, chopped
lemon wedges, to garnish
celery, cucumber and watercress, to serve

Heat butter and oil in a frying pan. Add pork steaks and fry for 3 minutes on each side.

Cover and cook gently for 15 minutes, turning occasionally. Remove pork steaks from pan and keep warm in a shallow flameproof dish. Add onion and garlic to pan and cook for 5 minutes.

Add mustard and wine to pan, stir well, then bring to the boil and boil for 1½ minutes. Stir in cream and heat through gently, then season with salt and pepper. Spoon mixture over pork steaks and sprinkle with chopped Mozzarella cheese. Cook under grill for 5 minutes until cheese is melted and bubbling. Serve hot, garnished with lemon wedges, with a salad of celery, cucumber and watercress.

Serves 4.

CHILLI BEAN TACOS

2 tablespoons olive oil
500 g (1 lb) pork sausagemeat, crumbled
1 onion, chopped
1 clove garlic, crushed
1/2 teaspoon ground cumin
1 teaspoon hot chilli powder
1 tomato, skinned and chopped
3 tablespoons tomato purée (paste)
1/2 a red pepper (capsicum), seeded and diced
315 g (10 oz) can kidney beans, drained
salt
8 taco shells
thick sour cream, paprika, lettuce leaves and radish
    roses, to serve

Preheat oven to 180C (350F/Gas 4). Heat oil
in a saucepan. Add sausagemeat, onion,
garlic, cumin and chilli powder and fry gently
for 5 minutes, stirring to break up
sausagemeat. Add tomato, tomato purée
(paste), red pepper (capsicum) and kidney
beans. Stir well and cook gently for 15
minutes, stirring frequently to prevent
mixture sticking. Season with salt.

Meanwhile, heat taco shells in the oven,
following packet instructions. Fill hot taco
shells with sausagemeat mixture. Top each
one with a spoonful of thick sour cream and
sprinkle with paprika. Serve with lettuce
leaves and radish roses.

Serves 4-8.

SCANDINAVIAN SALAD

155 ml (5 fl oz/²⁄₃ cup) malt vinegar
9 teaspoons granulated sugar
1 tablespoon Pickling Spice, see page 13
4 fresh herrings, cleaned and filleted
315 ml (10 fl oz/1¼ cups) thick sour cream
3 tablespoons mayonnaise
2 teaspoons wholegrain or Dijon mustard
1 onion, halved and thinly sliced
1 green eating apple
1 red eating apple
red lettuce leaves, to serve
sprigs of dill, to garnish

Put vinegar and 155 ml (5 fl oz/²⁄₃ cup) water
in a saucepan. Add sugar and spice.

Bring to the boil, stirring to dissolve sugar.
Boil for 2 minutes, then leave to cool. Strain
and discard spices. Cut herring fillets into 1
cm (½ in) wide strips and place in a dish.
Pour over cold marinade. Cover and
marinate for several hours or overnight.

Drain herring strips from marinade. Put sour
cream, mayonnaise, mustard and sliced
onion in a bowl and mix well. Quarter apples,
remove cores and slice thinly (do not peel).
Add sliced apples and herrings to bowl and
mix together gently until coated with
dressing. Arrange a border of lettuce leaves in
a serving bowl and spoon herring mixture
into the centre. Garnish with sprigs of dill
and serve chilled.

Serves 4.

TANGY DRUMSTICKS

1 small onion, chopped
1 tablespoon clear honey
1 clove garlic, crushed
3 tablespoons corn oil
3 tablespoons tomato ketchup (sauce)
1 tablespoon tomato purée (paste)
2 teaspoons Worcestershire sauce
1 teaspoon chilli sauce
2 pinches of Five-Spice Powder, see page 12
8 chicken drumsticks
cress and slices of lemon, to garnish

In a small saucepan, mix together onion, honey, garlic, 2 tablespoons oil, tomato ketchup (sauce) and purée (paste).

Add Worcestershire sauce, chilli sauce and five-spice powder and simmer, uncovered, for 5 minutes, stirring occasionally. Blend mixture to a smooth purée in a blender or food processor. Add remaining oil and stir well.

Arrange chicken drumsticks in a roasting tin. Brush with marinade and leave to marinate for 1 hour. Preheat oven to 200C (400F/Gas 6). Bake in oven for 35-40 minutes, turning and brushing frequently with marinade juices. Serve hot or cold, garnished with cress and lemon slices.

Serves 4.

PORK & PEPPERS

3 pinches of Five-Spice Powder, see page 12
2 tablespoons dry sherry or sake
2 tablespoons light soy sauce
1 clove garlic, crushed
2.5 cm (1 in) piece fresh root ginger, peeled and
   chopped
500 g (1 lb) pork tenderloin, cut into thin strips
2 onions
1 red pepper (capsicum), seeded
1 green pepper (capsicum), seeded
4 tablespoons corn oil
90 g (3 oz) button mushrooms, sliced
6 canned whole water chestnuts, sliced
2 teaspoons cornflour
155 ml (5 fl oz/⅔ cup) chicken stock
leek and spring onion curls, to garnish

In a bowl, mix together five-spice powder,
sherry or sake, soy sauce, garlic and ginger.
Add pork, stir well and marinate for 30
minutes. Cut onions into eighths and
separate into layers. Cut peppers (capsicums)
into thin strips. Heat 2 tablespoons oil in a
large frying pan or wok. Drain pork from
marinade (reserving marinade), add to pan
and stir-fry for 5 minutes. Remove from pan
and keep warm.

Add remaining oil to pan. Add onions,
peppers (capsicums), mushrooms and water
chestnuts and stir-fry for 3 minutes. Add
mixture to pork. Blend cornflour with
reserved marinade and 2 tablespoons stock.
Add remaining stock to pan and bring to the
boil. Add cornflour mixture and cook for 2
minutes, stirring all the time. Return pork
and vegetables to pan and heat through,
stirring all the time. Serve hot, garnished
with leek and spring onion curls.

Serves 4.

— CLAM & PRAWN CHOWDER —

60 g (2 oz/¼ cup) butter
1 large onion, chopped
2 sticks celery, chopped
2 potatoes, diced
1½ teaspoon fennel seeds
6 teaspoons plain flour
1 teaspoon paprika
470 ml (15 fl oz/1¾ cups) chicken stock
315 g (10 oz) can baby clams, drained
125 g (4 oz) peeled prawns, thawed if frozen
1 red pepper (capsicum), seeded and diced
125 g (4 oz) frozen sweetcorn, thawed
155 ml (5 fl oz/⅔ cup) single (light) cream
salt and pepper
sprigs of dill, to garnish

Melt butter in a saucepan. Add onion, celery, potatoes and fennel seeds and cook gently for 5 minutes, stirring frequently. Blend in flour and cook for 1 minute. Stir in paprika and stock and bring to the boil, stirring.

Reduce heat and simmer, covered, for 15 minutes, stirring occasionally. Add clams, prawns, red pepper (capsicum) and sweetcorn and simmer for a further 5 minutes. Stir in cream and season with salt and pepper. Serve hot, garnished with dill.

Serves 4.

Variation: Omit paprika and add 1 teaspoon Curry Powder, see page 12. Add 1 tablespoon chopped fresh parsley or coriander just before serving.

CREOLE JAMBALAYA

2 tablespoons olive oil
250 g (8 oz) piece ham, diced
250 g (8 oz) chorizo sausage, sliced
1 large Spanish onion, chopped
3 cloves garlic, crushed
1/2 teaspoon dried thyme
2 tablespoons chopped fresh parsley
375 ml (12 fl oz/1 1/2 cups) boiling chicken stock
315 g (10 oz) long-grain rice
1/4 teaspoon cayenne pepper
1 teaspoon Tabasco sauce
440 g (14 oz) can tomatoes
1 green pepper (capsicum), seeded and diced
2 tablespoons dry white wine
tomato and sprigs of thyme, to garnish

Heat oil in a saucepan. Add ham, chorizo sausage and onion and fry gently for 3 minutes. Add garlic, thyme and parsley and stir well, then add stock, rice, cayenne and Tabasco sauce and mix well. Add tomatoes and break up with a spoon. Bring mixture to the boil, stir well, then cover and simmer gently for 15 minutes.

Add green pepper (capsicum) and wine, stir well, then cover and continue cooking for a further 8 minutes or until liquid is absorbed. Fluff up with a fork and serve hot, garnished with tomato and thyme.

Serves 4-6.

Variations: Add 125 g (4 oz) peeled prawns (thawed, if frozen) to mixture 5 minutes before the end of cooking time.

For a more fiery flavour, increase cayenne and Tabasco sauce, according to taste.

STEAK AU POIVRE

1 ½ teaspoons green peppercorns
1 teaspoon black peppercorns
1 teaspoon white peppercorns
4 rump steaks, each weighing about 185 g (6 oz)
45 g (1 ½ oz/9 teaspoons) unsalted butter
few drops Tabasco sauce
few drops Worcestershire sauce
2 tablespoons brandy
3 tablespoons double (thick) cream
salt
sauté or jacket baked potatoes and green salad, to serve

Coarsely crush all peppercorns in a pestle and mortar.

Sprinkle crushed pepper over both sides of steaks, pressing in well with palm of hand. Set aside for 30 minutes. Melt 15 g (½ oz/3 teaspoons) butter in a large frying pan and heat until foaming. Add steaks and cook for 2-3 minutes, then turn and cook other sides for 2-3 minutes. (This timing gives medium-rare steaks, so adjust cooking time to suit personal preference). Turn steaks once again and top each one with 7 g (¼ oz/1½ teaspoons) butter and sprinkle with a few drops Tabasco sauce and Worcestershire sauce.

Pour over brandy and allow to heat through for a few seconds. Set it alight and remove from heat. When flames subside, lift steaks from pan and arrange on a warmed serving plate and keep warm. Add cream to pan, stir well and heat through for 1 minute, scraping up sediment from pan. Season with salt and spoon mixture over steaks. Serve at once with sauté or jacket baked potatoes and a green salad.

Serves 4.

CHEESE CHILLI BURGERS

2 tablespoons olive oil
2 onions, finely chopped
2 cloves garlic, crushed
250 g (8 oz) can tomatoes
100 g (3½ oz) can green chillies in brine
1 tablespoon chilli relish
½ teaspoon cumin seeds
500 g (1 lb) lean ground beef
salt and pepper
2 tablespoons corn oil
4 slices Gruyére cheese
shredded lettuce
4 warmed baps, split
raw onion rings

In a saucepan, heat olive oil. Add 1 chopped onion and garlic cloves and fry gently for 5 minutes. Purée tomatoes in a blender or food processor. Drain and chop chillies. Add tomatoes, chillies, chilli relish and cumin seeds to pan. Stir well, then cover and simmer for 10 minutes, stirring occasionally.

Put beef into a bowl. Add remaining onion and salt and pepper. Mix well together. Divide into 4 portions and shape each into a 10.5 cm (4½ in) round burger. Heat corn oil in a large frying pan. Add burgers and fry for 5-6 minutes on each side. Top each with a slice of cheese. Arrange lettuce on base of each bap. Place a burger on each and top with chilli sauce and onion rings. Cover with lids and serve hot.

Serves 4.

VEGETABLE COUSCOUS

250 g (8 oz) couscous
4 tablespoons olive oil
2 onions, coarsely chopped
1 large aubergine (eggplant), diced
500 g (1 lb) acorn squash, seeded and diced
2 carrots, sliced
1 teaspoon Harissa, see page 13
2 tomatoes, skinned and chopped
2 tablespoons tomato purée (paste)
470 ml (15 fl oz/2 cups) vegetable stock
410 g (13 oz) can chick peas, drained
2 courgettes (zucchini), sliced
60 g (2 oz/⅓ cup) sultanas or raisins
2 tablespoons chopped fresh parsley
sprig of coriander or parsley, to garnish

Put couscous in a bowl with 470 ml (15 fl oz/2 cups) water. Leave to soak for 15 minutes until water is absorbed. Heat oil in a saucepan. Add onions, aubergine (egg plant), squash and carrots and fry for 5 minutes, stirring frequently. Stir in harissa, tomatoes, tomato purée (paste) and stock. Bring to the boil and stir well. Line a large metal sieve or colander with muslin or all-purpose kitchen cloth and place over pan.

Put couscous into sieve. Cover whole pan with foil to enclose steam, then simmer for 20 minutes. Add chick peas, courgettes (zucchini) and sultanas or raisins to pan, stir well, then replace sieve and fluff up couscous with a fork. Cover again with foil and simmer for a further 20 minutes. Spread couscous on a large serving dish and fluff up with a fork. Add parsley to mixture in pan and spoon mixture over couscous. Serve hot, garnished with sprig of coriander or parsley.

Serves 4-6.

— CURRIED SCALLOP CREAMS —

8 large fresh scallops
1 slice of lemon
½ bay leaf
750 g (1½ lb) potatoes, cut into even-sized pieces
67 g (2¾ oz/generous ¼ cup) butter
salt and pepper
90 g (3 oz) button mushrooms, sliced
2 shallots, finely chopped
½-1 teaspoon Curry Powder, see page 12
30 g (1 oz/¼ cup) plain flour
3 tablespoons double (thick) cream
2 tablespoons chopped fresh parsley
fresh bay leaves, lemon and lime twists and sprigs of
    dill, to garnish

Wash scallops, pat dry and cut in slices.

Put scallops in a saucepan with 315 ml (10 fl oz/1¼ cups) water, lemon slice and bay leaf. Simmer gently for 20 minutes. Strain, reserving liquor. Discard lemon and bay leaf. Make up liquor to 315 ml (10 fl oz/1¼ cups) with water, if necessary. Meanwhile, cook potatoes in boiling, salted water until tender. Drain, return to pan and shake over low heat for a few seconds to dry off. Mash with 22 g (¾ oz/4½ teaspoons) butter and salt and pepper. Beat well and cool slightly. Transfer to a piping bag fitted with a large star nozzle.

Pipe a border of potato around 4 scallop dishes. Melt remaining butter in a pan. Add mushrooms, shallots and curry powder. Cook for 2 minutes. Stir in flour and cook for 1 minute. Add reserved liquor and bring to boil. Reduce heat and simmer for 2 minutes, stirring. Remove from heat. Stir in cream, scallops, parsley, salt and pepper. Spoon into dishes and place under a preheated grill for 4-5 minutes until hot. Garnish with bay leaves, lemon and lime twists and dill.

Serves 4.

CHILLI CON CARNE

2 tablespoons olive oil
625 g (1¼ lb) lean minced beef
2 onions, chopped
1 clove garlic, crushed
2 sticks celery, chopped
2 teaspoons hot chilli powder
1 teaspoon cumin seeds
440 g (14 oz) can tomatoes
2 tablespoons tomato purée (paste)
470 g (15 oz) can red kidney beans, drained
1 teaspoon salt
boiled rice, thick sour cream, diced avocado and raw
    onion rings, to serve

Preheat oven to 180C (350F/Gas 4). Heat oil in flameproof casserole.

Add minced beef, onions, garlic and celery and fry gently for 5 minutes, stirring occasionally. Add chilli powder and cumin and cook gently for 2 minutes. Add tomatoes, and break up with a spoon. Stir in tomato purée (paste) and kidney beans. Bring to the boil, stirring.

Cover and bake in the oven for 1 hour, stirring occasionally. Season mixture with salt. Serve the chilli over boiled rice in individual bowls and top each serving with a spoonful of thick sour cream, diced avocado and raw onion rings.

Serves 4.

Note: To prevent avocado discolouring, toss in lemon juice.

For a more fiery flavour, add 3 teaspoons chilli powder at step 2.

NASI GORENG

250 g (8 oz/1½ cups) long-grain rice
3 tablespoons corn oil
2 onions, halved and sliced
2 cloves garlic, crushed
2 small fresh green chillies, seeded and chopped
185 g (6 oz) pork tenderloin, diced
185 g (6 oz) skinned chicken breast (fillets), diced
¼ teaspoon hot chilli powder
1 teaspoon paprika
2 tablespoons light soy sauce
125 g (4 oz) peeled prawns, thawed if frozen
salt
1 egg
7 g (¼ oz/1½ teaspoons) butter
prawn crackers, to serve

Cook rice in boiling, salted water for 12 minutes. Drain and rinse well, then drain again. Heat oil in a large frying pan. Add onions, garlic and chillies and fry for 2 minutes. Add pork and chicken and fry gently for 10 minutes until cooked. Add chilli powder, paprika, soy sauce, prawns and rice and cook for 5-6 minutes until piping hot, stirring all the time. Season with salt.

Turn mixture into a warm serving dish and keep warm, while preparing omelette topping. Whisk egg with 1 teaspoon water. Melt butter in a frying pan. Add egg mixture and swirl pan to give a thin, even mixture. Cook over gentle heat for 2-3 minutes until set and lightly golden underneath. Turn omelette out onto a board. Roll up and cut into slices. Arrange slices of omelette on top of rice mixture. Serve hot with prawn crackers.

Serves 4.

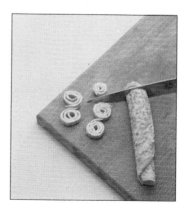

INDIAN CHICKEN PIES

30 g (1 oz/6 teaspoons) butter
60 g (2 oz) button mushrooms, chopped
1 onion, chopped
2 teaspoons Garam Masala, see page 12
410 g (13 oz/3¼ cups) plain flour
155 ml (5 fl oz/⅔ cup) chicken stock
315 g (10 oz) cooked chicken, diced
60 g (2 oz) frozen sweetcorn, thawed
salt and pepper
90 g (3 oz/⅓ cup) block margarine, diced
90 g (3 oz/⅓ cup) lard, diced
beaten egg, to glaze
sprig of parsley and tomato slices, to garnish

Melt butter in a saucepan. Add mushrooms, onion and garam masala and cook 2 minutes.

Stir in 30 g (1 oz/¼ cup) flour and cook for 1 minute, then stir in stock and bring to the boil, stirring. Reduce heat and cook for 2 minutes, stirring all the time. Remove from heat and stir in chicken, sweetcorn and salt and pepper.

Sift remaining flour into a bowl. Add ¼ teaspoon salt and rub in margarine and lard finely until mixture resembles breadcrumbs. Add 4 tablespoons cold water and mix to form a fairly firm dough. Knead gently until smooth.

Preheat oven to 190C (375F/Gas 5). Cut off two-thirds of pastry and cut into 4 equal portions. Roll out each portion to a round large enough to line an individual 12.5 cm (5 in) diameter, loose-based, fluted flan tin, allowing pastry to overlap top rim slightly. Press pastry well into flutes but do not trim top edge at this stage. Cut remaining one-third pastry into 4 equal pieces and roll out each piece to a round large enough to cover pies.

Spoon cold chicken mixture into pastry-lined flan tins and smooth over surfaces. Dampen edges of pastry in tins and cover with pastry lids. Seal edges well together and trim by pressing pastry edges firmly all the way round with the flat blade of a knife – this cuts through pastry and gives a neat, sealed edge. Make a small hole in centre of each pie. Re-roll pastry trimmings and cut out leaves to decorate pies. Brush surfaces of pies with beaten egg, then decorate with leaves and brush these with egg.

Place flan tins on a preheated baking sheet and bake in the oven for 40-45 minutes until pastry is golden brown and filling is heated through. Leave pies to cool before carefully removing from tins. Serve cold, garnished with parsley and tomato slices.

Serves 4.

Variation: Use Curry Powder, see page 12, instead of Garam Masala, if preferred, or try a mixture of each.

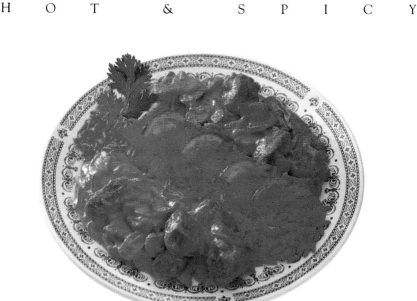

— LAMB & MUSHROOM KORMA —

3 tablespoons corn oil
1 large onion, coarsely chopped
4 cm (1½ in) piece fresh root ginger, peeled and
   chopped
2 cloves garlic, crushed
1 teaspoon ground cumin
1 teaspoon ground coriander
4 cardamom pods, crushed and seeds removed
½ teaspoon turmeric
750 g (1½ lb) lean lamb, cubed
315 ml (10 fl oz/1¼ cups) natural yogurt
185 g (6 oz) button mushrooms, sliced
1 teaspoon lemon juice
salt and pepper
lime slices and sprigs of coriander, to garnish
nan bread and saffron rice, to serve

Heat oil in a saucepan. Add onion and fry gently until lightly golden. Add ginger, garlic, cumin, coriander, cardamom seeds and turmeric and fry gently for 2 minutes, stirring. Add lamb and fry until browned all over, stirring frequently. Stir in yogurt and bring to the boil.

Stir well, then cover and cook gently for 45 minutes, stirring occasionally. Add the mushrooms, re-cover and continue cooking for a further 15 minutes until lamb is tender and yogurt is absorbed. Stir in lemon juice, season with salt and pepper and cook, uncovered, for 5 minutes. Garnish with lime slices and coriander sprigs, and serve hot with nan bread and saffron rice.

Serves 4.

CHILLI PEPPER PIZZA

3 tablespoons olive oil
1 onion, quartered and sliced
1 clove garlic, crushed
250 g (8 oz) can tomatoes
1 tablespoon tomato purée (paste)
½ teaspoon dried oregano
125 g (4 oz/1 cup) plain flour
125 g (4 oz/1 cup) plain wholewheat flour
¼ teaspoon salt
1 teaspoon easy blend dried yeast
155 ml (5 fl oz/⅔ cup) hand-hot water
100 g (3½ oz) can green chillies in brine
185 g (6 oz) Mozzarella cheese, chopped
60 g (2 oz) pepperoni salami sticks, sliced
8 black or green olives
tomato roses and sprigs of parsley, to garnish

Heat 2 tablespoons oil in a saucepan. Add onion, garlic, tomatoes, tomato purée (paste) and oregano. Stir well to break up tomatoes, then simmer, uncovered, for 10-15 minutes until well thickened. Leave to cool. Preheat oven to 190C (375F/Gas 5). Put flours, salt and yeast into a bowl and mix well. Add water and mix to form a dough. Knead well, then roll out to a round large enough to line a lightly greased 25 cm (10 in) pizza tray.

Brush surface of dough with a little of the remaining oil and cover with tomato mixture. Drain and chop chillies and sprinkle on top. Scatter with chopped cheese and drizzle with remaining oil. Bake in the oven for 25 minutes. Add sliced pepperoni and olives to pizza and continue cooking for a further 10 minutes. Serve hot, cut into wedges, garnished with tomato roses and sprigs of parsley.

Serves 2 (as a meal) or 4 (as a snack).

INDONESIAN BEEF

750 g (1½ lb) topside of beef, cut into slices
3 tablespoons corn oil
1 large Spanish onion, sliced
1 clove garlic, crushed
1 teaspoon ground ginger
1 teaspoon ground cumin
1 teaspoon ground coriander
1 teaspoon chilli seasoning
60 g (2 oz/⅔ cup) desiccated coconut
2 teaspoons light soft brown sugar
1 tablespoon lemon juice
315 ml (10 fl oz/1¼ cups) beef stock
thin slivers of red pepper (capsicum) and green chilli
and small onion rings, to garnish

Cut slices of topside into 1 cm (½ in) thick strips. Heat oil in a saucepan. Add onion and garlic and fry gently until soft. Add meat and fry, stirring, until browned all over.

Add spices to pan and cook for 2 minutes. Add remaining ingredients, except garnish, and stir well. Simmer gently, uncovered, for 30-35 minutes, stirring occasionally, until mixture is thickened and dry. Stir mixture more frequently towards the end of cooking time to prevent it sticking. Serve hot, garnished liberally with thin slivers of red pepper (capsicum) and green chilli and small onion rings.

Serves 4.

SPANISH OMELETTE

1 tablespoon olive oil
15 g (½ oz/3 teaspoons) butter
1 onion, chopped
1 clove garlic, crushed
1 red pepper (capsicum), seeded and diced
90 g (3 oz) green cabbage, finely shredded
4 rashers streaky bacon, chopped
1 teaspoon fenugreek
½ teaspoon ground coriander
4 eggs, beaten
salt and pepper
60 g (2 oz/½ cup) grated Cheddar cheese
strips of red pepper (capsicum) and sprigs of parsley, to
garnish
salad and crusty bread, to serve

Heat oil and butter in a 17.5-20 cm (7-8 in) frying pan. Add onion, garlic, red pepper (capsicum), cabbage and bacon and fry over gentle heat for 5 minutes, stirring occasionally. Add fenugreek and coriander and stir well.

Whisk eggs with 1 tablespoon cold water and salt and pepper, then pour into pan. Swirl pan to ensure an even coating. Cook over gentle heat for 3-4 minutes until mixture is golden brown underneath. Sprinkle surface with grated cheese and place pan under a preheated grill and cook until mixture is set on top and cheese has melted. Cut into 4 portions and serve hot, garnished with strips of red pepper (capsicum) and sprigs of parsley, with salad and crusty bread.

Serves 4.

VEGETARIAN MEDLEY

125 g (4 oz/¾ cup) whole green lentils
125 g (4 oz/¾ cup) split peas
2 leeks, cut into 0.5 cm (¼ in) slices
2 courgettes (zucchini), cut into 0.5 cm (¼ in) slices
2 carrots, thinly sliced
2 sticks celery, thinly sliced
1 onion, coarsely chopped
1 clove garlic, crushed
30 g (1 oz/6 teaspoons) ghee
½ teaspoon turmeric
1 teaspoon mustard seeds
2 teaspoons Garam Masala, see page 12
salt
celery leaves and slices of lemon, to garnish

Soak lentils and split peas overnight. Drain lentils and peas and put into a saucepan. Add 625 ml (20 fl oz/2½ cups) cold water, bring to the boil and boil for 10 minutes. Add vegetables and garlic to pan, then cover and cook gently for 10 minutes.

Meanwhile, melt ghee in a pan. Add turmeric, mustard seeds and garam masala and cook gently for 2 minutes until seeds begin to pop. Stir into lentil mixture and continue cooking for a further 15 minutes or until vegetables and lentils are tender and liquid has been absorbed. Season with salt, garnish with celery leaves and slices of lemon and serve hot.

Serves 4.

CHICKEN TANDOORI

1 teaspoon dry mustard
5 cm (2 in) piece fresh root ginger, peeled and chopped
½ teaspoon cumin seeds
½ teaspoon ground coriander
½ teaspoon turmeric
1 teaspoon lemon juice
¼ teaspoon hot chilli powder
2 teaspoons tomato purée (paste)
90 ml (3 fl oz/⅓ cup) corn oil
155 ml (5 fl oz/⅔ cup) natural yogurt
8 chicken drumsticks, skinned
lemon and lime twists and sprigs of parsley, to garnish

In a bowl, mix first 7 ingredients.

Add tomato purée (paste) and oil, a little at a time, mixing well to form a smooth sauce. Stir in yogurt. Prick drumsticks several times with a cocktail stick and put into a shallow dish. Pour marinade over drumsticks and turn drumsticks in mixture. Cover and leave to marinate overnight in refrigerator.

Preheat grill. Arrange drumsticks in grill pan and cook for 30-35 minutes until cooked through, turning and basting frequently to ensure even browning and cooking. Serve hot, garnished with lemon and lime twists and sprigs of parsley.

Serves 4.

FALAFEL

410 g (13 oz) can chick peas, drained
1 onion, quartered
2 cloves garlic
125 g (4 oz) fresh white bread
¼ teaspoon cumin seeds
4 small dried red chillies, crushed
1 tablespoon chopped fresh parsley
salt and pepper
1 egg, beaten
45 g (1½ oz/⅓ cup) golden breadcrumbs
vegetable oil for deep frying
4 warmed pitta bread, shredded lettuce, sliced onion
    and sliced tomato, to serve

Put chick peas, onion, garlic, bread, cumin seeds and chillies in a blender or food processor. Process ingredients until smooth, then turn mixture into a bowl. Add parsley, salt and pepper and beaten egg and mix well. Form into 8 balls and coat in breadcrumbs. Flatten each one slightly to form oval shapes.

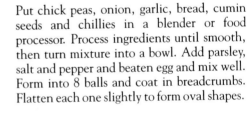

Half-fill a deep fat pan or fryer with oil. Heat to 190C (375F) or until a cube of day-old bread browns in 40 seconds. Fry the falafel, a few at a time, for 3 minutes until golden brown. Drain on absorbent kitchen paper. Cut each pitta bread in half and open out to form pockets. Put a falafel in each pocket with a little shredded lettuce and a few slices raw onion and tomato. Serve hot.

Makes 8.

CEYLONESE CURRY

2 large onions
5 cm (2 in) piece fresh root ginger, peeled
2 cloves garlic
5 tablespoons corn oil
2½-3 tablespoons Curry Powder, see page 12
750 g (1½ lb) boneless chicken breasts, skinned
4 teaspoons plain flour
375 ml (12 fl oz/1½ cups) chicken stock
1 red or green pepper (capsicum), seeded
2 sticks celery, sliced
½ teaspoon cumin seeds
90 g (3 oz) button mushrooms, if desired
22 g (¾ oz) creamed coconut, chopped
2 large tomatoes, peeled, seeded and sliced
toasted shredded coconut and chervil sprigs, to garnish

Put one of the onions into a blender or food processor. Chop ginger and add with garlic and 2 tablespoons water. Blend until very finely chopped. Heat 3 tablespoons oil in a saucepan. Add onion and ginger mixture and curry powder and fry for 2 minutes, stirring all the time. Cut chicken into bite-sized cubes and add to pan. Fry until sealed all over. Stir in flour and cook for 1 minute, then stir in stock and bring to the boil. Cover and simmer gently for 15 minutes.

Meanwhile, peel and slice remaining onion and separate into rings. Dice pepper (capsicum). Heat remaining oil in a frying pan. Add celery, onion rings, red pepper (capsicum), cumin seeds and mushrooms, if desired, and fry gently for 4 minutes. Add mixture to saucepan and continue cooking for a further 15 minutes. Stir in creamed coconut, then add tomato slices and heat through. Serve hot, garnished with shredded coconut and chervil.

Serves 4.

BARBECUE SAUCE

3 tablespoons corn oil
1 small onion
1 clove garlic, crushed
½ teaspoon dry mustard
2 tablespoons malt vinegar
1 tablespoon Worcestershire sauce
2 tablespoons light soft brown sugar
3 tablespoons tomato ketchup (sauce)
½ teaspoon chilli seasoning
185 ml (6 fl oz/¾ cup) chicken stock
sprig of parsley, to garnish

Heat oil in a small saucepan. Add onion and garlic and cook gently for 2 minutes, stirring frequently.

Stir in mustard, vinegar, Worcestershire sauce, sugar, tomato ketchup (sauce), chilli seasoning and chicken stock. Bring to the boil.

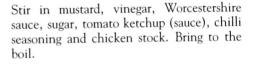

Cover and simmer sauce gently for 7-8 minutes until slightly thickened. Serve hot as a sauce, garnished with sprigs of parsley, with beefburgers, hot dogs or fried chicken. Or, if preferred, allow to cool and use to brush over meats, poultry and fish while baking or grilling.

Makes 315 ml (10 fl oz/1¼ cups).

WINE & PEPPER SAUCE

30 g (1 oz/6 teaspoons) unsalted butter
2 shallots, finely chopped
1 tablespoon brandy
125 ml (4 fl oz/½ cup) dry white wine
125 ml (4 fl oz/½ cup) chicken stock
2 teaspoons green peppercorns, coarsely crushed
3 tablespoons double (thick) cream
1 tablespoon chopped fresh parsley
sprig of parsley, to garnish

Melt butter in a frying pan. Add shallots and cook gently for 3 minutes. Add brandy to pan and allow to heat through for a few seconds, then set it alight and when flames subside, add wine to pan.

Stir in stock and peppercorns and boil rapidly for 2-3 minutes until quantity is slightly reduced.

Remove from heat and stir in cream and parsley. Return to medium heat and heat through for 2-3 minutes, stirring all the time. Serve hot, garnished with a sprig of parsley, with steaks, veal or fish dishes.

Makes 185 ml (6 fl oz/¾ cup).

INDIAN DRESSING

1 tablespoon corn oil or ghee
1 small onion, finely chopped
2 teaspoons Curry Powder, see page 12
¼ teaspoon cayenne pepper
1 cm (½ in) piece fresh root ginger, peeled and chopped
155 ml (5 fl oz/⅔ cup) mayonnaise
1 tablespoon tomato purée (paste)
1 tablespoon Mango Chutney, see page 89
3 tablespoons single (light) cream or natural yogurt
cucumber slices, cucumber skin and sprig of parsley, to
 garnish

Heat oil or ghee in a saucepan. Add onion, curry powder, cayenne and ginger and cook gently for 5 minutes, stirring frequently.

Remove from heat and cool. Put mayonnaise, tomato purée (paste) and mango chutney into a blender or food processor. Add cooled onion mixture and cream or yogurt and blend until smooth.

Turn mixture into a serving bowl. Chill for at least 1 hour before serving. Garnish with cucumber slices and skin and parsley. Serve as an accompaniment to cold meats and salads.

Makes 220 ml (7 fl oz/1 cup).

Note: The consistency of this dressing may be thinned with the addition of a little more single cream or yogurt, if preferred. Dressing will keep, in a covered container in refrigerator for several days.

SPICY CHILLI SAUCE

1 clove garlic
1 Spanish onion, quartered
2 fresh green chillies, seeded
2 tablespoons corn oil
½ teaspoon ground ginger
250 g (8 oz) can tomatoes
60 g (2 oz/⅓ cup) seedless raisins
1 tablespoon lemon juice
1 tablespoon dark soy sauce
30 g (1 oz/2 tablespoons) light soft brown sugar
salt and pepper
sprig of parsley, to garnish

In a blender or food processor, finely chop garlic, onion and chillies.

Heat oil in a saucepan. Add onion mixture and ginger and cook gently for 3 minutes. Add tomatoes and break up with a spoon. Stir in raisins, lemon juice, soy sauce, sugar and 315 ml (10 fl oz/1¼ cups) water.

Bring to the boil, then reduce heat and simmer, uncovered, for 15 minutes. Blend to a smooth purée in a blender or food processor. Reheat and season with salt and pepper. Serve hot, garnished with a sprig of parsley, with grilled steak or fried chicken.

Makes 625 ml (20 fl oz/2½ cups).

Note: This sauce is also delicious served with grilled white fish.

TANGY MUSTARD SAUCE

45 g (1½ oz/9 teaspoons) butter
1 small onion, finely chopped
30 g (1 oz/¼ cup) plain flour
280 ml (9 fl oz/1 cup) chicken stock
155 ml (5 fl oz/⅔ cup) milk
1 bay leaf
1 teaspoon wholegrain mustard
2 teaspoons dry mustard
1 tablespoon wine vinegar
1 teaspoon caster sugar
salt and pepper
bay leaves, to garnish

Melt butter in a saucepan. Add onion and cook gently for 2 minutes. Stir in flour.

Cook for 1 minute. Stir in stock and bring to the boil, stirring. Reduce heat and simmer for 2 minutes, stirring all the time. Add milk and bay leaf, stir well and cook for 2 minutes.

Blend mustards smoothly with vinegar and sugar. Add mixture to pan and season with salt and pepper, then heat through for 2-3 minutes. Remove bay leaf. Serve sauce hot, garnished with bay leaves, with smoked sausage, rabbit or fish dishes.

Makes 470 ml (15 fl oz/1¾ cups).

Note: This recipe gives a good coating sauce, so if a pouring sauce is desired, simply add a little more stock or milk.

COCONUT SAUCE

90 g (3 oz/1 cup) desiccated coconut
410 ml (13 fl oz/1⅔ cups) boiling water
3 tablespoons corn oil
1 onion, quartered and thinly sliced
1 clove garlic, crushed
3 teaspoons Curry Powder. see page 12
½ teaspoon turmeric
½ teaspoon ground coriander
½ teaspoon hot chilli powder
3 teaspoons cornflour
1 tablespoon lemon juice
1 large tomato, skinned and seeded
½ small green pepper (capsicum), seeded
salt

Put coconut and boiling water into a blender
or food processor and blend for 45 seconds.
Pass mixture through a fine sieve, pressing
coconut firmly to extract liquor. Heat oil in a
saucepan. Add onion, garlic, curry powder,
turmeric, coriander and chilli powder and fry
gently for 3 minutes, stirring.

Add coconut milk and bring to the boil.
Cover and simmer gently for 5 minutes.
Blend cornflour with lemon juice and add to
pan. Bring to the boil and cook for 2 minutes,
stirring all the time. Cut tomato and green
pepper (capsicum) into thin slivers and add
to sauce. Cook gently for 5 minutes. Season
with salt. Serve hot with grilled steak,
chicken or stir-fry dishes.

Makes 560 ml (18 fl oz/2¼ cups).

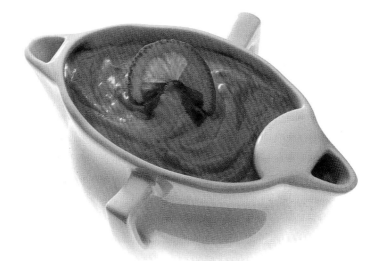

LEMON HOLLANDAISE

60 ml (2 fl oz/¼ cup) lemon juice
1 teaspoon black peppercorns
3 blades of mace
2 large egg yolks
125 g (4 oz/½ cup) butter, at room temperature
3 good pinches of cayenne pepper
thin slice of lemon and paprika, to garnish

Put lemon juice, peppercorns and mace into a small saucepan. Bring to the boil and boil until liquid is reduced by half. Put egg yolks into a bowl with 15 g (½ oz/3 teaspoons) butter and beat well together.

Strain the hot lemon liquid onto butter mixture, beating well all the time with a wooden spoon. Return to pan and place over a very low heat. Gradually add small pieces of remaining butter, whisking really well all the time, until sauce is thickened and smooth. (If mixture gets too hot at this stage it will curdle and separate. To prevent this happening, keep removing pan from heat whilst beating in butter to ensure gentle cooking.)

Add cayenne pepper to sauce and mix well. Turn mixture into a warm serving dish. Garnish with a thin slice of lemon and a sprinkling of paprika. Serve warm or cold with poached salmon, asparagus or globe artichokes.

Makes 155 ml (5 fl oz/⅔ cup).

Note: Remember that this rich egg and butter-based sauce requires great care during cooking to achieve the delicious result.

PIQUANT ORIENTAL SAUCE

2 tablespoons corn oil
1 onion, quartered and thinly sliced
1 carrot, cut into fine matchstick strips
½ green pepper (capsicum), seeded and cut into thin strips
4 cm (1½ in) piece fresh root ginger, peeled and chopped
3 pinches of Five-Spice Powder, see page 12
250 g (8 oz) can pineapple slices
1 tablespoon granulated sugar
1 tablespoon dark soy sauce
1 tablespoon dry sherry
1 tablespoon malt vinegar
1½ tablespoons tomato ketchup (sauce)
3 teaspoons cornflour
155 ml (5 fl oz/⅔ cup) chicken stock

Heat oil in a saucepan. Add onion, carrot, green pepper (capsicum) and ginger and stir-fry for 3 minutes. Add five-spice powder and remove from heat. Drain pineapple slices, reserving juice. Make juice up to 155 ml (5 fl oz/⅔ cup) with water. Cut 2 slices of pineapple into thin pieces (use the remaining pineapple in a fruit salad).

In a bowl, mix together sugar, soy sauce, sherry, vinegar, tomato ketchup (sauce) and pineapple juice. Add to pan together with pineapple pieces. Blend cornflour smoothly with a little stock. Add to pan and bring to the boil, stirring all the time. Reduce heat and simmer for 2 minutes, stirring. Serve hot with fried chicken, pork steaks or shellfish.

Makes 625 ml (20 fl oz/2½ cups).

Note: Garnish with a few pineapple leaves if they are available.

ROAST PEPPER RELISH

1 yellow, 1 red and 1 green pepper (capsicum), halved and seeded
1 onion, quartered and thinly sliced
90 ml (3 fl oz/¹⁄₃ cup) corn oil
2 tablespoons lemon juice
1 teaspoon wholegrain mustard
1 clove garlic, crushed
¹⁄₂ teaspoon Garam Masala, see page 12
1 ¹⁄₂ teaspoons caster sugar
salt and pepper
sprigs of coriander, to garnish

Preheat oven to 200C (400F/Gas 6). Put peppers (capsicums) in a roasting tin.

Bake in the oven for 30 minutes or until skins begin to blister and blacken. Cool peppers (capsicums), then peel away thin skins. Cut peppers (capsicums) into quarters and slice into thin strips. Put peppers (capsicums) into a shallow dish. Sprinkle with onion.

Put remaining ingredients into a screw-top jar and shake vigorously until well blended. Pour mixture over peppers (capsicums) and marinate for several hours, stirring occasionally. Serve chilled, garnished with sprigs of coriander, as an accompaniment to game pies, cold meats or crusty bread and cheese.

Serves 4.

Note: This colourful relish keeps well in the refrigerator for up to 3 days.

MANGO CHUTNEY

3 mangoes (barely-ripe)
2 tablespoons corn oil
2 cm (¾ in) piece fresh root ginger, peeled and chopped
1 clove garlic, crushed
1 teaspoon salt
½ teaspoon hot chilli powder
¼ teaspoon cumin seeds
½ teaspoon fenugreek
315 ml (10 fl oz/1¼ cups) malt vinegar
90 g (3 oz/½ cup) seedless raisins
1 tablespoon lemon juice
250 g (8 oz/1½ cups) light soft brown sugar
sprig of parsley, to garnish

Slice mangoes in half by cutting lengthwise close to stones on either side.

Peel and cut flesh into 0.3 cm (⅛ in) thick slices. Also cut away as much mango flesh as possible from around stones, without including any fibrous parts of stone. Heat oil in a large saucepan. Add sliced mangoes, ginger, garlic, salt, chilli powder, cumin seeds and fenugreek. Cook gently for 2 minutes, stirring.

Stir in vinegar, raisins, lemon juice and sugar. Heat slowly to dissolve sugar, then bring to the boil and simmer, uncovered, for 35-40 minutes or until liquid thickens and becomes syrupy and mango looks translucent. Stir frequently during cooking. Spoon mixture into jars. Cover tightly and label. It can be eaten straight away or stored in a cool, dry, dark place. Serve, garnished with parsley, as an accompaniment to curries, or with cold meats and cheeses.

Makes 1.25 kg (2½ lb).

PICCALILLI

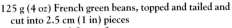

125 g (4 oz) French green beans, topped and tailed and
  cut into 2.5 cm (1 in) pieces
250 g (8 oz) cauliflower flowerets
250 g (8 oz) small pickling onions, peeled
250 g (8 oz) piece cucumber, diced
125 g (4 oz/½ cup) cooking salt
1 teaspoon turmeric
3 teaspoons dry mustard
½ teaspoon ground ginger
90 g (3 oz/⅓ cup) granulated sugar
470 ml (15 fl oz/1¾ cups) distilled malt vinegar
4 teaspoons cornflour
cucumber, to garnish

Layer all vegetables in a colander with salt.

Leave to stand overnight. Rinse well under
cold running water and drain thoroughly.
Mix turmeric, mustard, ginger and sugar with
all but 60 ml (2 fl oz/¼ cup) vinegar and
blend well. Put mixture into a saucepan and
add vegetables. Simmer gently for 9-10
minutes until vegetables are part-cooked but
still crisp.

Blend cornflour to a smooth paste with
remaining vinegar. Add to pan and mix well.
Bring to the boil and cook for 3 minutes,
stirring carefully all the time to prevent
damaging vegetables. Spoon mixture into
jars. Cover tightly and label. It can be eaten
straight away or stored in a cool, dry, dark
place. Serve, garnished with cucumber, with
cold pies, salads or sandwiches.

Makes 1.5 kg (3 lb).

— YOGURT TOMATO COOLER —

1 tablespoon corn oil
2 cloves garlic, crushed
½ teaspoon cumin seeds
220 ml (7 fl oz/1 cup) natural yogurt
½ teaspoon paprika
2 firm tomatoes, finely chopped
4 spring onions, finely chopped
2 tablespoons chopped fresh mint
salt and pepper
sprigs of mint, to garnish
hot buttered nan or pitta bread, to serve

Heat oil in a small saucepan. Add garlic and cumin seeds and cook very gently for 2 minutes. Remove from heat and cool.

Put yogurt into a bowl. Add cooled garlic mixture and paprika and stir well. Add tomatoes, spring onions and chopped mint and season with salt and pepper.

Turn mixture into a serving bowl and chill for several hours before serving, garnished with sprigs of fresh mint. Serve as an accompaniment to curries or as a tasty snack with hot buttered nan or pitta bread.

Serves 4.

Variation: Omit tomatoes. Add 1 peeled, seeded and finely chopped, or grated, cucumber to the mixture instead.

PICKLED RED CABBAGE

1 kg (2 lb) red cabbage
45 g (1½ oz/9 teaspoons) cooking salt
2 tablespoons Pickling Spice, see page 13
1.2 litres (40 fl oz/5 cups) distilled malt vinegar
2 teaspoons caraway seeds

Quarter cabbage and discard centre stalk. Shred cabbage finely. Layer cabbage in a colander with salt and leave overnight.

Put pickling spice and vinegar into a saucepan. Bring to the boil and boil for 3 minutes, then remove from heat and leave to cool. When cold, strain and reserve.

Rinse cabbage well under cold running water. Drain thoroughly and mix with caraway seeds. Pack cabbage into four 500 g (1 lb) jars. Pour cold, spiced vinegar over to cover cabbage completely. Cover tightly and label. Store in a cool, dry, dark place for at least 5 days before serving. Serve as an accompaniment to cold meats and poultry.

Makes 2 kg (4 lb).

Note: Use cabbage within 2 months; if left longer cabbage loses its crispness.

INDIAN APPLE CHUTNEY

500 g (1 lb) cooking apples
500 g (1 lb) onions, chopped
2 cloves garlic, crushed
125 g (4 oz/¾ cup) sultanas
2 teaspoons salt
375 g (12 oz/1½ cups) granulated sugar
625 ml (20 fl oz/2½ cups) malt vinegar
¼ teaspoon cayenne pepper
¼ teaspoon ground cumin
¼ teaspoon ground ginger
1 teaspoon mustard seeds
¼ teaspoon dry mustard
1 tablespoon tomato purée (paste)
sprig of parsley, to garnish

Peel, core and coarsely chop apples.

Put apples, onions, garlic, and sultanas into a saucepan. Add salt, sugar, vinegar and spices and mix well. Heat gently, stirring to dissolve sugar.

Bring to the boil and simmer for 30 minutes, stirring occasionally. Stir in tomato purée (paste) and continue cooking for a further 7-8 minutes until mixture is of a thick consistency with very little free liquid. Stir mixture frequently during this time. Spoon mixture into three 500 g (1 lb) jars. Cover tightly and label. Store in a cool, dry, dark place. Store for at least 3 weeks. Serve with curries or with crusty bread and cheese. Garnish with parsley.

Makes 1.5 kg (3 lb).

SPICY PICKLED PLUMS

1 kg (2 lb) firm ripe plums
4 allspice berries
4 small dried red chillies
four 2.5 cm (1 in) cinnamon sticks
6 whole cloves
4 blades of mace
785 ml (25 fl oz/3 cups) distilled malt vinegar
750 g (1½ lb/3 cups) granulated sugar
sprig of mint, to garnish

Prick plums several times with a cocktail stick. Half-fill two 1 kg (2 lb) jars with plums.

Add 2 allspice berries, 2 chillies, 2 cinnamon sticks, 3 cloves and 2 blades mace to each jar. Add remaining plums to fill jars. Put vinegar and sugar into a saucepan and bring to the boil, stirring to dissolve sugar. Boil for 5 minutes.

Pour hot vinegar into jars to cover plums. Cool, then cover tightly and label. Store in a cool, dry, dark place for at least 1 month before serving. Serve, garnished with sprig of mint, with cold meats and salads.

Makes 2 kg (4 lb).

ANCHOVY SPREAD

60 g (2 oz) can anchovy fillets, drained
1 tablespoon milk
30 g (1 oz/6 teaspoons) butter, softened
30 g (1 oz) Bel Paese cheese
1 teaspoon lemon juice
3 pinches of cayenne pepper
3 pinches of ground nutmeg
¼ teaspoon Tabasco sauce
2 teaspoons capers, drained and finely chopped
fingers of hot toast, to serve
radish slices and watercress sprigs, to garnish

Put anchovies into a bowl with the milk.
Leave to soak for 30 minutes. Drain well,
then pat dry on absorbent kitchen paper.

Chop anchovies finely and put into a bowl
with the butter and cheese. Mix well
together. Add lemon juice, cayenne, nutmeg
and Tabasco sauce.

Blend to a smooth purée in a blender or food
processor, scraping mixture down from sides
of bowl between blends. Add capers and mix
well. Spread thinly onto fingers of hot toast
and garnish with radish slices and watercress
sprigs.

Serves 4-6.

Note: This mixture will keep in the
refrigerator for up to 5 days.

WINE-GLAZED ORANGES

125 g (4oz/½ cup) granulated sugar
185 ml (6 fl oz/¾ cup) red wine
4 whole cloves
2 teaspoons cassia bark, broken into small pieces
1 small piece dried root ginger
4 large oranges
grated orange peel, to decorate
single (light) cream, to serve

Put sugar and 185 ml (6 fl oz/¾ cup) water into a saucepan and heat slowly, stirring to dissolve sugar. Add wine, cloves, cassia and ginger. Bring to the boil and boil until mixture is slightly thickened and syrupy. Cool for 5 minutes.

Meanwhile, prepare oranges. Peel oranges, using a sharp knife, removing all bitter white pith. Cut oranges into 0.5 cm (¼ in) thick slices and place in a shallow dish. Strain wine syrup over oranges. Cover and chill for several hours or overnight, turning slices occasionally in syrup.

Using cocktail sticks, secure orange slices together to form neat, whole oranges and place in a serving dish. Pour wine syrup over oranges. Decorate with orange peel and serve with cream.

Serves 4.

Note: If preferred, serve oranges in slices rather than as whole oranges.

PINEAPPLE CREAM PEARS

1 tablespoon lemon juice
4 large, firm pears
4 pieces crystallized ginger, halved
30 g (1 oz/6 teaspoons) butter
1 tablespoon light soft brown sugar
155 ml (5 fl oz/⅔ cup) pineapple juice
155 ml (5 fl oz/⅔ cup) double (thick) cream
toasted, flaked almonds and fresh bay leaves, to
    decorate

Preheat oven to 190C (375F/Gas 5). Fill a
bowl with cold water and add lemon juice.
Peel and halve the pears. Cut away stalks and
remove cores, using a teaspoon. Place
prepared pears in bowl of lemon water.

Lightly grease a shallow ovenproof dish. Pat
pears dry on absorbent kitchen paper. Put a
piece of crystallized ginger into the 'well' of
each pear half. Arrange pears, cut-sides
down, in the ovenproof dish.

Put butter into a saucepan with sugar and
pineapple juice and heat gently to dissolve
sugar. Add cream and boil for 5 minutes. Pour
sauce over pears. Cover and bake in oven for
1 hour until pears are tender and sauce has
thickened. Baste pears with sauce several
times during cooking. Arrange pears on a
warm serving plate and spoon sauce over.
Decorate with toasted, flaked almonds and
bay leaves to represent pear leaves. Serve
hot.

Serves 4.

MELON & GINGER BASKET

1 large, ripe Honeydew melon
60 ml (2 fl oz/¼ cup) orange juice
1-2 pieces stem ginger, thinly sliced
2 tablespoons stem ginger syrup
freshly grated nutmeg
2 kiwi fruit, peeled, halved and sliced
8 lychees, peeled and stones removed
8 strawberries, halved
8 black grapes, halved and pips removed
ice cream, to serve
sprig of mint, to decorate

Cut a thin slice off one of the rounded sides of melon (not pointed ends), so melon will stand level on serving plate.

Make 2 cuts on either side of a central strip, to form a handle, about 2 cm (¾ in) wide. Continue cutting halfway down melon then cut from base of handle around either side of fruit so these two wedges can be lifted away to form a basket shape. Cut away flesh from inside the handle. Remove seeds from melon. Using a small melon scoop, scoop out flesh in neat balls and place in a bowl. (Alternatively, cut flesh into neat pieces.) Neaten edge of melon basket.

Add orange juice, sliced stem ginger and syrup and nutmeg to taste to melon balls and stir lightly. Add kiwi fruit, lychees, strawberries and grapes and mix lightly together. Spoon mixture into melon and pile fruits up attractively. Cover and chill before serving with ice cream. Decorate with mint.

Serves 4-6.

Variation: Use any fresh fruits of your choice, such as cherries, pineapple, peaches, figs, nectarines.

— LEMON GINGER SYLLABUBS —

315 ml (10 fl oz/1¼ cups) double (thick) cream
90 g (3 oz/⅓ cup) caster sugar
finely grated peel of 1 lemon
2 tablespoons lemon juice
2 pieces stem ginger, chopped
1 egg white
2 kiwi fruit, peeled, quartered and sliced
4 teaspoons stem ginger syrup
twists of lemon and slices stem ginger, to decorate
dainty sweet biscuits, to serve

Whip cream with sugar until it begins to thicken. Add lemon peel and juice and whisk until thick and velvety.

Fold in chopped stem ginger. Whisk egg white stiffly and fold into cream mixture. Place kiwi fruit in bases of 4 glasses. Sprinkle each one with stem ginger syrup. Top with cream mixture. Chill for 2 hours.

Decorate each one with a twist of lemon and slices of stem ginger. Serve with dainty sweet biscuits.

Serves 4.

Variation: Stoned cherries, sliced peaches or nectarines may be used instead of kiwi fruit, if preferred.

BERRIES & PEPPER SAUCE

1 lemon
250 g (8 oz/1 cup) granulated sugar
315 ml (10 fl oz/1¼ cups) orange juice
1 tablespoon green peppercorns, coarsely crushed
500 g (1 lb) strawberries
strawberry or mint leaves, to decorate, if desired
single (light) cream, to serve

Finely grate peel from lemon and put into a saucepan. Squeeze juice from lemon and reserve. Add sugar and 155 ml (5 fl oz/⅔ cup) water to pan and heat gently, stirring until sugar dissolves.

Bring to the boil and boil until syrup turns a light caramel colour. Remove from heat and, holding pan handle with a cloth (as mixture will splutter), add orange and lemon juices. Heat gently, stirring to dissolve caramel.

Stir in peppercorns and boil again for 3-4 minutes until slightly thickened and syrupy. Allow to cool for 2 minutes. Arrange strawberries in a serving dish, then spoon hot syrup over them and serve at once, decorated with strawberry leaves or mint, if desired, with single (light) cream.

Serves 4.

GLAZED APPLE TART

185 g (6 oz/1½ cups) plain flour
pinch of salt
140 g (4½ oz/½ cup plus 3 teaspoons) butter
3 tablespoons caster sugar
1 egg yolk
4 green eating apples (such as Granny Smith)
finely grated peel of ½ a lemon
½ teaspoon cornflour
½ teaspoon ground cinnamon
2 pinches of ground nutmeg
5 tablespoons apricot jam
2 tablespoons lemon juice
sprig of mint, to decorate
cream, to serve

Sift flour and salt into a bowl.

Add 125 g (4 oz/½ cup) butter and rub in finely until mixture resembles breadcrumbs. Stir in 1 tablespoon caster sugar and bind together with egg yolk and 2 teaspoons cold water. Knead gently until smooth and chill for 15 minutes. Preheat oven to 190C (375F/ Gas 5). Melt remaining butter and use to grease a 20 cm (8 in) shallow sandwich cake tin. Sprinkle with remaining caster sugar. Peel, core and cut apples into fairly thin slices. Arrange a layer of apple slices in over-lapping circles over base of tin.

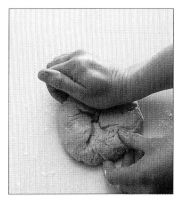

Mix remaining slices with lemon peel, cornflour and spices. Pack on top of arranged slices. Roll out pastry to a round large enough to cover surface and fit into tin. Prick with a fork. Bake in oven for 40 minutes until pastry is golden brown. Carefully turn out onto a warm serving plate. Put jam and lemon juice into a saucepan and heat gently until melted, stirring. Spoon over apple. Serve hot or cold, decorated with a sprig of mint, with cream.

Serves 6-8.

SPICY PROFITEROLES

75 g (2½ oz/½ cup, plus 6 teaspoons) plain flour
1 teaspoon ground cinnamon
67 g(2¼ oz/¼ cup, plus 1½ teaspoons) butter, diced
2 eggs, beaten
315 ml (10 fl oz/1¼ cups) double (thick) cream
1 tablespoon icing sugar
2 teaspoons coffee essence
125 g (4 oz) plain (dark) chocolate, broken up
2 tablespoons Tia Maria
2 tablespoons golden syrup
2 teaspoons caster sugar

Preheat oven to 200C (400F/Gas 6). Lightly grease 2 baking sheets.

Sift flour and ½ teaspoon cinnamon onto a piece of greaseproof paper. Put 155 ml (5 fl oz/⅔ cup) water in a saucepan. Add 52 g (1¾ oz/10½ teaspoons) butter and heat gently until butter melts. Do not allow water to boil before butter melts. Rapidly bring to boil, remove from heat and add flour all at once and stir quickly, using a wooden spoon, to form a smooth mixture. Return pan to medium heat for a few seconds and beat well until dough forms a smooth ball and leaves sides of pan clean.

Remove from heat and cool slightly. Gradually add beaten egg, a little at a time, beating well after each addition to form a smooth, shiny dough. Transfer dough to a piping bag fitted with a 2 cm (¾ in) plain nozzle. Pipe 24 small balls onto baking sheets.

Bake in the oven for 20 minutes, then reduce oven temperature to 180C (350F/Gas 4) and continue cooking for a further 15-20 minutes until buns are well risen, crisp and sound hollow when tapped on bases. Make a slit in the side of each one to allow steam to escape. Cool on a wire rack.

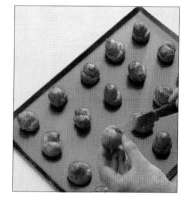

Whip cream with icing sugar and coffee essence until thick. Transfer to a piping bag fitted with a small star nozzle and pipe cream into choux buns. (Alternatively, use a teaspoon to fill buns with cream.) Arrange profiteroles in a pyramid-shape on a serving dish.

Melt chocolate and remaining butter in the top of a double boiler or a bowl set over a pan of simmering water. Stir in Tia Maria and syrup and continue stirring until sauce is smooth and coats back of a spoon. Spoon sauce over profiteroles and leave to set for a few minutes. Mix remaining cinnamon with caster sugar and sprinkle over profiteroles.

Serves 6.

BAKLAVA

60 g (2 oz/¼ cup) caster sugar
155 g (5 oz/1⅓ cups) blanched chopped almonds
90 g (3 oz/¾ cup) chopped walnuts
1½ teaspoons ground cinnamon
½ teaspoon Mixed Spice, see page 13
500 g (1 lb) filo pastry
200 g (7 oz/1 cup) unsalted butter, melted
220 g (12 oz/1½ cups) granulated sugar
4 large pieces cassia bark
6 whole cloves
strip of lemon peel
2 tablespoons clear honey

In a bowl, mix together caster sugar, almonds, walnuts, cinnamon and spice.

Preheat oven to 160C (325F/Gas 3). Grease a 25 x 32.5 cm (10 x 13 in) roasting tin. Line base with a sheet of filo pastry, trimming it to fit. Brush with melted butter and add a further 7 sheets of filo pastry, trimming and brushing each one with butter. Sprinkle over half nut mixture, then cover with 4 sheets pastry, trimming and brushing each one with melted butter. Sprinkle remaining nut mixture on top and cover with 5 more sheets of filo, trimming and brushing each one with melted butter. Spread any remaining butter on top.

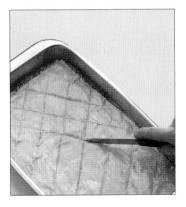

Using a sharp knife, cut through top layers of pastry to make about 25 diamond-shaped pieces. Bake in oven for 1 hour until golden brown, covering with foil, if necessary, to prevent overbrowning. Leave to cool in tin. Put granulated sugar and 345 ml (11 fl oz/1⅓ cups) water in a large saucepan. Add cassia, cloves, lemon peel and honey and heat gently, stirring. Boil for 5 minutes, then strain over baklava. Leave overnight.

Makes about 25 pieces.

CORNISH SAFFRON CAKE

three 0.05 g packets saffron strands
1 tablespoon boiling water
90 g (3 oz/⅓ cup) caster sugar
250 ml (8 fl oz/1 cup) hand-hot water
3 teaspoons dried yeast
750 g (1½ lb/5 cups) strong plain white flour
¼ teaspoon salt
185 g (6 oz/¾ cup) lard
125 g (4 oz/½ cup) butter
250 g (8 oz/1⅔ cups) currants

Put a piece of foil in grill pan. Place saffron on foil and spread thinly. Switch grill to low and gently dry saffron (do not discolour) for 3-4 minutes.

Place saffron in a small bowl and crush to a fine powder. Add 1 tablespoon boiling water and leave to soak for 8 hours. Next day, dissolve 1 teaspoon of caster sugar in 60 ml (2 fl oz/¼ cup) of hand-hot water. Add yeast, whisk and leave for 10-15 minutes until frothy. Put flour, salt, lard and butter into a bowl and rub in finely. Mix in remaining sugar and currants. Stir saffron into remaining water and add to bowl. Stir in yeast and mix to form a dough. Knead lightly, then cover and leave in a warm place to rise until doubled in bulk.

Lightly grease two 1 kg (2lb) loaf tins. Knead dough and divide in half. Press each piece to a rectangle. Roll up and put into tins with joins underneath. Press into corners. Cover and prove at room temperature until risen to top of tins (this may take 2-3 hours). Preheat oven to 190C (375F/Gas 5). Bake in oven 35-45 minutes until cooked. Cover with foil if necessary, to prevent overbrowning. Cool on wire rack. Leave until the next day before slicing.

Makes 2 cakes.

FROSTED GINGERBREAD

250 g (8 oz/2 cups) plain flour
¼ teaspoon salt
½ teaspoon Mixed Spice, see page 13
1½ teaspoons ground ginger
1 teaspoon bicarbonate of soda
90 g (3 oz/¼ cup) golden syrup
90 g (3 oz/¼ cup) black treacle
90 g (3 oz/⅓ cup) block margarine
90 g (3 oz/½ cup) dark soft brown sugar
2 eggs, beaten
220 ml (7 fl oz/1) cup milk
90 g (3 oz) full fat soft cheese
185 g (6 oz/1 cup) icing sugar
slices of crystallized ginger, to decorate

Preheat oven to 160C (325F/Gas 3). Grease an 18 x 28 cm (7 x 11 in) shallow baking tin and line base with greased, greaseproof paper, allowing paper to stand 2.5 cm (1 in) above sides of tin. Sift flour, salt, mixed spice, ginger and bicarbonate of soda into a bowl. Put golden syrup, black treacle, margarine and brown sugar into a saucepan and heat gently until melted. Stir mixture into bowl and add eggs and milk. Stir well together until evenly mixed.

Pour into prepared tin and bake in the oven for 45-50 minutes until well risen and cooked through. Leave to cool in tin, then turn out and remove lining paper. In a bowl, soften cheese, then gradually sift in icing sugar. Mix well to make a soft creamy mixture. Spread over cold cake. Using blade of a knife, form a rippled effect on icing sugar. Decorate with crystallized ginger. Serve cut into chunky squares or slices.

Makes 12 squares or slices.

JAMAICAN RUM CAKE

185 g (6 oz/1½ cups) self-raising flour
1½ teaspoons baking powder
1 teaspoon Mixed Spice, see page 13
185 g (6 oz/¾ cup) soft tub margarine
3 eggs
185 g (6 oz/¾ cup) caster sugar
6 teaspoons cocoa powder
6 teaspoons hot water
125 g (4 oz/½ cup) granulated sugar
2 cinnamon sticks
4 tablespoons dark rum
15 g (½ oz/6 teaspoons) slivered almonds
185 g (6 oz) plain (dark) chocolate, broken up
whipped cream

Preheat oven to 160C (325F/Gas 3).

Well grease a 1.2 litre (40 fl oz/5 cup) fluted or plain ring tin and dust lightly with flour. Sift flour, baking powder and mixed spice into a bowl. Add margarine, and eggs and caster sugar. Blend cocoa with hot water and add to bowl. Beat well with wooden spoon for 2 minutes (or for only 1 minute, if using an electric mixer) until well blended. Turn mixture into prepared tin. Bake in oven for 1¼ hours or until well risen and beginning to shrink away from edge of tin. Carefully turn cake out onto a wire rack and leave to cool.

Put granulated sugar and 155 ml (5 fl oz/⅔ cup) water into a pan, add cinnamon and heat, stirring. Boil for 5 minutes. Remove from heat, add rum and discard cinnamon. Put cake on a plate. Spoon over syrup and leave for 2 hours. Stud top with almonds. Melt chocolate in the top of a double boiler or a bowl set over a pan of simmering water. Spoon chocolate over cake. Leave to set, then decorate around base of cake with piped, whipped cream.

Serves 10-12.

BRANDY SNAPS

60 g (2 oz/¼ cup) butter
60 g (2 oz/ ¼ cup) demerara sugar
60 g (2 oz/2 tablespoons) golden syrup
60 g (2 oz/½ cup) plain flour
pinch of salt
2 pinches of Mixed Spice, see page 13
½ teaspoon ground ginger
½ teaspoon lemon juice
155 ml (5 fl oz/⅔ cup) double (thick) cream
1 teaspoon icing sugar
few drops vanilla essence
small strawberries, sliced

Preheat oven to 160C (325F/Gas 3). Well grease 3 baking sheets.

Put butter, sugar and syrup into a saucepan and heat gently until butter has melted and sugar dissolved. Cool slightly. Sift flour, salt, mixed spice and ginger onto mixture, add lemon juice and stir well together. Put teaspoonfuls of mixture onto prepared baking sheets, spacing them well apart to allow for spreading. Bake in the oven (one sheet at a time) for 6-8 minutes until golden. Leave to cool on baking sheet for 2 minutes.

Using a palette knife, remove brandy snaps from baking sheet, one at a time, and roll around the handle of a wooden spoon. Leave to set before removing from handle. Just before serving, whip cream with icing sugar and vanilla essence until thick. Transfer cream to a piping bag fitted with a small star nozzle and pipe cream into the ends of each brandy snap. Add strawberry slices to each end and serve at once.

Makes 12.

GERMAN PEPPER COOKIES

1 egg
125 g (4 oz/½ cup) caster sugar
125 g (4 oz/1 cup) plain flour
pinch of salt
½ teaspoon ground cinnamon
¼ teaspoon ground white pepper
¼ teaspoon Mixed Spice, see page 13
3 teaspoons cornflour
½ teaspoon baking powder
finely grated peel of 1 lemon
2 tablespoons chopped mixed citrus peel
icing sugar for sprinkling

In a bowl, whisk egg and sugar together until light and fluffy.

Sift flour, salt, cinnamon, pepper, mixed spice, cornflour and baking powder onto mixture. Add lemon peel and mixed citrus peel and stir well together. Chill for 1 hour.

Preheat oven to 180C (350F/Gas 4). Lightly grease 2 or 3 baking sheets. Form mixture into 16 small balls and place, well apart on baking sheets. Bake in the oven for 20 minutes until well risen and lightly golden. Cool on a wire rack. Sprinkle with icing sugar. Store for several days before serving, to allow time for flavours to mellow.

Makes 16.

PEANUT BUTTER COOKIES

125 g (4 oz/¹/₂ cup) soft tub margarine
140 g (4¹/₂ oz) crunchy peanut butter
125 g (4 oz/¹/₂ cup) caster sugar
125 g (4 oz/³/₄ cup) light soft brown sugar
1 large egg, beaten
185 g (6 oz/1¹/₂ cups) plain flour
¹/₂ teaspoon baking powder
³/₄ teaspoon bicarbonate soda
good pinch of salt
¹/₂ teaspoon Mixed Spice, see page 13
¹/₄ teaspoon ground cinnamon
2 good pinches of freshly grated nutmeg
halved glacé cherries and blanched almonds,
    to decorate

Lightly grease 2 or 3 baking sheets. In a bowl, beat margarine with peanut butter, sugars and egg until well combined. Sift flour with baking powder, bicarbonate of soda, salt and spices. Add to mixture and mix well. Divide into 25 equal portions and shape into balls. Place, spaced well apart, on baking sheets. Flatten to 5 cm (2 in) rounds by pressing with a fork, first one way, then the other. Put a halved glacé cherry onto centre of 13 cookies and 12 blanched almonds onto remainder. Chill for 30 minutes.

Preheat oven to 190C (375F/Gas 5). Bake cookies in the oven for 10-12 minutes or until cooked through, but not hard. Leave to cool on baking sheets for 5 minutes, then cool completely on a wire rack. Store in an airtight tin for up to 2 weeks.

Makes 25.

Note: These cookies should be slightly chewy in the centre. However, if you prefer them crisp, do not chill mixture, but instead cook straight away.

ICED COFFEE CREAM

6 teaspoons instant coffee
4 teaspoons light soft brown sugar
90 ml (3 fl oz/⅓ cup) boiling water
¼ teaspoon ground cinnamon
few pinches of Mixed Spice, see page 13
375 ml (12 fl oz/1½ cups) chilled milk
few drops vanilla essence
5 tablespoons double (thick) cream
8 ice cubes
4 small scoops vanilla ice cream
½ teaspoon drinking chocolate
cinnamon sticks and slices of lime, to decorate

In a jug, dissolve coffee and sugar in boiling water. Add cinnamon and mixed spice.

Add 155 ml (5 fl oz/⅔ cup) cold water, stir well. Add chilled milk, vanilla essence to taste and cream and whisk lightly until evenly combined.

Put 2 ice cubes into each of 4 glasses. Half-fill with coffee mixture, then add a scoop of ice cream and top up with remaining coffee. Sprinkle with drinking chocolate and serve at once with long-handled spoons. Decorate each one with a cinnamon stick and slices of lime.

Serves 4.

Variations: For a sweeter version, add more sugar to taste at step 1. If liked, top each glass with a little whipped cream.

GLÜHWEIN

1 orange
8 whole cloves
60 g (2 oz/ ¼ cup) granulated sugar
3 cinnamon sticks
freshly grated nutmeg
3 blades of mace
1 litre (32 fl oz /4 cups) red wine
slices of orange and cinnamon sticks, to decorate

Stud orange with cloves and put into a saucepan. Add 315 ml (10 fl oz/ 1¼ cups) water, sugar, cinnamon, nutmeg to taste and mace.

Heat gently, stirring to dissolve sugar. Bring to the boil, then reduce heat and simmer for 5 minutes.

Add red wine and heat through gently for a few minutes. Strain and serve hot in heatproof glasses. Float orange slices on top and decorate with cinnamon sticks.

Serves 8-10.

PINA COLADA PUNCH

1 piece dried root ginger, bruised with spoon
1 tablespoon light soft brown sugar
1 tablespoon cassia bark, broken into small pieces
2 China tea bags
60 g (2 oz/⅔ cup) desiccated coconut
315 ml (10 fl oz/1 ¼ cups) boiling water
470 ml (15 fl oz/1 ¾ cups) pineapple juice
155 ml (5 fl oz/⅔ cup) light rum or gin
cocktail cherries, pieces of pineapple and pineapple
  leaves, to decorate

Put ginger, sugar and cassia bark into a saucepan.

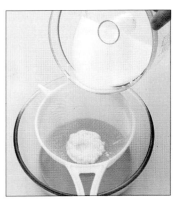

Add 155 ml (5 fl oz/⅔ cup) water and bring to the boil. Cover and simmer for 5 minutes. Remove from heat and add tea bags. Leave to soak for 5 minutes, then strain into a bowl. Put coconut and boiling water into a blender or food processor and blend for 1 minute. Leave to stand for 5 minutes, then strain into tea mixture, pressing coconut well to extract all moisture.

Add pineapple juice and chill for 1 hour. Add rum or gin and stir well. Serve over crushed ice in tall glasses. Decorate glasses with cocktail sticks threaded with cocktail cherries, pieces of pineapple and pineapple leaves. Add a swizzle stick to each glass.

Serves 4-6.

Variation: Add more rum or gin for a stronger flavoured drink.

NEGUS

1 bottle ruby port
1 tablespoon light soft brown sugar
finely grated peel of 1 lemon
4 tablespoons lemon juice
¼ teaspoon freshly grated nutmeg
¼ teaspoon ground cinnamon
4 whole cloves
625 ml (20 fl oz/2½ cups) boiling water
thin strips of lemon peel, to decorate

Put port into a saucepan and heat gently (do not allow to boil).

Add sugar, grated lemon peel and juice and spices. Stir well together and leave over a very low heat for 10 minutes. Remove cloves.

Add boiling water and serve hot in heatproof glasses, decorated with strips of lemon peel.

Serves 10-12.

HOT MULLED CIDER

1 large cooking apple
14 whole cloves
3 cinnamon sticks
6 allspice berries
¼ teaspoon freshly grated nutmeg
30 g (1 oz/2 tablespoons) light soft brown sugar
1 litre (32 fl oz/4 cups) medium dry cider
30 g (1 oz/6 teaspoons) butter
slices of red apple and sprigs of mint, to decorate

Stud apple with cloves. Cut apple in half and put, cut-sides down, into a saucepan. Add 155 ml (5 fl oz/⅔ cup) water, cinnamon, allspice, nutmeg and sugar.

Cover and simmer gently for 20 minutes. Strain into a pan. Remove spices and press cooked apple through sieve into pan.

Add cider and butter and heat through gently. Serve hot in heatproof glasses with slices of red apple floating on top and decorated with sprigs of mint.

Serves 8-10.

GINGER BEER

finely grated peel and juice of 1 large lemon
5 teaspoons cream of tartar
500 g (1 lb/2 cups) granulated sugar
30 g (1 oz) fresh root ginger, peeled
30 g (1 oz) dried root ginger
2.25 litres (4 pints/10 cups) boiling water
15 g (½ oz/3 teaspoons) fresh yeast
1 slice of toast
sprigs of mint, lemon slices and strips of peel,
    to decorate

Put lemon peel, cream of tartar and sugar into a large bowl or clean plastic bucket. Crush fresh ginger and dried root ginger with a rolling pin and add to bowl.

Pour over boiling water and stir well until sugar dissolves. Add 2.25 litres (4 pints/10 cups) cold water and lemon juice and stir well. Spread yeast on toast and float (yeast-side down) on mixture. Cover with a clean cloth and leave in a warm place for 24 hours.

Strain ginger beer through muslin. Pour into clean, plastic fizzy drink bottles, filling each one only half-full (this allows room for mixture to effervesce on opening). Screw on lids tightly and leave in a cool place for 2-3 days before drinking. (Even if the ginger beer is not required at this stage, it is a wise precaution to open each bottle to allow excess air to escape.) Once opened, drink within 2 weeks. Serve, decorated with sprigs of mint, lemon slices and strips of peel.

Serves 15-20.

SHERBET

250 g (8 oz/1 cup) granulated sugar
2 cinnamon sticks
½ teaspoon whole cloves
8 green cardamons, lightly crushed
3 strips of lemon peel
½ teaspoon rose water
1-2 drops red food colouring, if desired
curls of lemon peel and rose petals, to decorate

Put 470 ml (15 fl oz/1¾ cups) water into a saucepan. Add sugar, cinnamon, cloves, cardamons and strips of lemon peel. Heat gently, stirring to dissolve sugar.

Bring to the boil, then reduce heat and simmer gently for 20-30 minutes until mixture is thickened and syrupy. Remove from heat.

Stir in rose water and colouring, if desired. Strain and leave to cool, then dilute with ice-cold water. Serve in glasses, decorated with curls of lemon peel and rose petals.

Serves 6-8.

SWEET LASSI

470 ml (15 fl oz/1¾ cups) natural yogurt
4 ice cubes
315 ml (10 fl oz/1¼ cups) ice-cold water
2 teaspoons lemon juice
2 tablespoons caster sugar
ice cubes, to serve
½ teaspoon cumin seeds, crushed
thin slices of lemon and sprigs of mint, to decorate

Put yogurt, 4 ice cubes and ice-cold water into a blender or food processor and blend for 30 seconds.

Add lemon juice and caster sugar and blend mixture again until thoroughly combined.

Pour mixture over ice cubes in 6 glasses and serve, sprinkled with crushed cumin seeds. Decorate each glass with a thin slice of lemon and a sprig of mint.

Serves 6.

— AUSTRIAN CHOCOLATE CUP —

90 g (3 oz) plain (dark) chocolate, broken up
finely grated peel of 1 small orange
¼ teaspoon ground cinnamon
375 ml (12 fl oz/1½ cups) milk
4 tablespoons double (thick) cream
grated chocolate, to serve
cinnamon sticks, to decorate

Put chocolate, orange peel, cinnamon and 3 tablespoons milk into a saucepan and heat very gently until melted, stirring frequently.

Add remaining milk and heat through gently until piping hot, stirring frequently. Whisk cream until softly peaking.

Pour hot chocolate into mugs or heatproof glasses. Top each one with a spoonful of whipped cream. Sprinkle with grated chocolate and add a cinnamon stick to each one for stirring.

Serves 2-3.

Note: Wind a curly strip of orange peel around each cinnamon stick for a pretty effect.

INDEX